SURVIVED

One Millimetre at a Time

Dr Pamela Dunn

Copyright © 2018 Pamela Dunn

All rights reserved. No part of this book may be reproduced in any form without permission from the publisher.

First Edition

Visit the author's website: www.survived.com.au

Disclaimer – please note:

I have tried to recreate events, locales and conversations from my memories of them. In order to maintain their anonymity in some instances I may have changed the names of individuals and places. I may have changed some identifying characteristics and details such as physical properties, occupations and places of residence.

Although the author and publisher have made every effort to ensure that the information in this book was correct at press time, the author and publisher do not assume and hereby disclaim any liability to any party for any loss, damage, or disruption caused by errors or omissions, whether such errors or omissions result from negligence, accident, or any other cause.

This book is not intended as a substitute for the medical advice of physicians. The reader should regularly consult a physician in matters relating to his/her health and particularly with respect to any symptoms that may require diagnosis or medical attention.

National Library of Australia Cataloguing in Publication Entry

ISBN: 978-0-6481857-1-0

DEDICATION

This book is dedicated to all of my patients that I have had the pleasure of working with as a health practitioner over the years.

Introduction

I am grateful to say that I am a proud survivor of Guillain Barre Syndrome (GBS). It has been a long road to recovery, and also very slow. They say that in order to recover from GBS, it is at a pace of one millimetre at a time. That is no exaggeration. I can now speak from experience and realise through the long, arduous road, that it has been an amazing revelation about how the human body can go through such a horrific process and come through on the other side. More important are the lessons that I have learned along the way.

I spent nearly 20 years as a chiropractor looking after patients and managing chiropractic practices before I was diagnosed with GBS. At that significant moment in August 2013, I found myself in a reversed role as a patient.

I feel that what I went through physically, mentally, and emotionally was not only profound, but penetrating to my consciousness as well. I was encouraged by other health professionals, family and friends to share my experience - that to keep it all to myself would be selfish.

It has taken me years to get the right words together in the form that brings me a sense of contentment. On reflection, I understood that timing was so relevant and the lessons unfolded one step at a time.

In a million years, I never thought that this could happen to me. And I'd like to share with you, that if it could happen to me, it could happen to anyone.

It is my hope that there is something in this book that may help you in your own life, no matter what challenge or tragic life event you may come across. It doesn't have to be GBS.

Please know that I am writing this from my heart, being authentic, real and raw. Raw as the nerves were when the myelin was stripped away through the process of GBS...

"Life will give you whatever experience is most helpful for the evolution of your consciousness."

~ Eckhart Tolle

Contents

Chapter One – GBS WTF 1

Chapter Two – I Am Not My Hair 23

Chapter Three – The Pain 37

Chapter Four – Letting Go 49

Chapter Five – The Power of the Mind 63

Chapter Six – Memories of ICU 79

Chapter Seven - Memories of Rehabilitation 99

Chapter Eight – Milestones 127

Chapter Nine – Up Close and Personal 139

'Survived' Essentials 148

About the Author 149

Acknowledgments 151

"There is no greater agony than bearing an untold story inside you."

~ Maya Angelou

Chapter One – GBS WTF

"It is during our darkest moments that we must focus to see the light."
~ Aristotle

A BIT OF BACKGROUND

GBS WTF is the original title I would like to have named this book. It deserves it.

Guillain Barre Syndrome (pronounced gee-yan-buh-rey), or GBS for short, is a rare, relatively unknown syndrome that most people haven't heard of. Unless you know someone who has had it, or you have unfortunately had it yourself, chances are you haven't heard of it. It's similar to Multiple Sclerosis (MS) except in MS the body slowly deteriorates with little to no chance of reversal; in GBS you hit rock bottom and have an opportunity to slowly get better and recover.

I knew of it because of my chiropractic background. I studied it in Neurology when I went to Chiropractic University. In the 5-year chiropractic program, it probably got about 10-15 minutes of a mention on the day in class. Ironically, I remember thinking at the time, "that would really be awful – to only be able to 'think & blink'." Almost 20 years later, I found myself in that exact situation.

GBS is an autoimmune disorder where the body's immune system attacks the nervous system and in turn demyelinates the neurons (nerve cells). Demyelination is when the myelin, or protective coating, is stripped from the nerves. The nerves need the myelin sheaths for the transmission of electrical impulses. When the nerves can't communicate with the brain on the superhighway from brain to spinal cord and back - then there are numerous complications that follow. The nervous system ends up in a state of extreme chaos, including paralysation.

A myriad of symptoms and treatments follow, depending on the severity and depending on the individual. I will share my personal experience throughout this book.

The irony here is the nervous system involvement. For me, as a chiropractor, this is the most important system of the body. Since I was a child of 9 years old, I dedicated my life's purpose to helping people by adjusting their spines and extremities to assist in relieving nerve interference. My GBS experience furthered my appreciation of the nervous system and human body even more.

I have never valued my health and wellbeing more than I do now, every single day. GBS has given me a new outlook on life, and I try to remember to take it day by day, which GBS has taught me literally...one millimetre at a time.

THE BEGINNING

My life was busy. My life had its stresses and strains, but doesn't everyone's? I felt I was managing it all pretty well. I was a daughter, sister, wife, friend and mother of a 16 year-old daughter at the time. I had a busy suburban chiropractic practice and a country chiropractic practice. I managed to fit in my friends on the social calendar and make time to enjoy life the best I could.

(Christmas 2012 – Mark, Marina and I)

Admittedly, I had been running on all cylinders but I thought that was normal. I was in my early 40s and felt I was juggling everything quite efficiently. I'm the type of person that doesn't complain, tries to keep a positive attitude, eat well, exercise, sleep well and generally look after myself the best I can. I have a very independent nature, and my family and friends would agree I can be quite stubborn too.

(April 2013 - 3 months before GBS diagnosis)

The weekend before I was diagnosed with GBS, I travelled to Sydney to attend a workshop and ended up having free time to have a long weekend by myself. I ended up having a wonderful time and enjoyed it immensely as I truly enjoy my own company. I saw aspects of this amazing city through different eyes. I was in a different place in my life compared to years ago when different priorities were taking up my time.

(July 2013 – weekend before GBS diagnosis)

I had some personal reflection time during the free time from the workshop that allowed me to do some soul searching and connect with nature.

In hindsight, I did have some pretty significant stressful events leading up to my diagnosis of GBS, yet I still believed that I was coping. I wasn't able to identify how much of an impact these events may or may not have had on my health. After all, I was eating well and exercising. Looking after the physical, but was I looking after the mental/emotional state?

So I put my metaphoric 'Superwoman cape' back on and got back to my 'normal' routine.

Flying back to Perth (29 July 2013), I had mixed feelings of not wanting to leave that day due to wanting more time in Sydney, versus getting back to the world that was so busy and hectic. Whilst I was happy to see my husband Mark and my daughter Marina, I was apprehensive about going back to work the very next day, even though I loved the drive out to my country practice and the people from the town.

I felt sluggish that Tuesday, but put it down to 'needing another day' to unwind from the trip before jumping back into it. As the years go by, I am reminded that this is becoming more and more important. My dear friend commented I looked tired but again I blamed it on 'jet lag' from travelling over east to Sydney and back over the weekend.

The next day (31 July 2013) was scheduled to be my last full

Wednesday in my chiropractic practice. I had organised a few weeks before to have that as the last full day, as in starting at 8:30am and finishing by 7:00pm. I was listening to my body and such a long day was becoming increasingly more difficult. I felt less than average that day and even though I went home at lunchtime and lay down for an hour, I still struggled that afternoon. I noticed that I had weird sensations in my legs from the knees down while I was standing and treating patients. These were weird sensations that I had never experienced before. Both legs were affected equally and I felt like I needed to sit down or even lay down, but kept going as there were patients scheduled.

When I finished with my last patients, I told the receptionist I was not feeling well and that I was going home to have a bath and go straight to bed. Thursday was my normal day off and whilst I had numerous errands and plans, I cancelled all of them and told myself I was staying home to rest and replenish the energy I was lacking. I did that but I didn't feel any better. In fact, I was slowly getting worse. Normally I would make some healthy soup, drink herbal teas, and take some Chinese herbs, thinking that I was getting a flu or cold, and rest. Usually 24 hours later I would be fine. Unfortunately this was not the case. I felt quite weak by that Thursday afternoon as well. A bit confused by this, I actually felt unable to go into the office the next day to see patients, and for the first time in my almost 20 year long career as a chiropractor, I had the receptionist cancel my patients due to my not being well enough to attend. Even when I slammed my foot in the door many years ago and broke my toe, I still went to the office with a swollen foot, limping to see patients. Some people may think that is ludicrous, but I know myself and I was capable then, but not this time.

Friday was no better. I lost count of how many cups of herbal tea that I had. I made miso soup, took some Chinese herbs to combat flu, yet I was growing weaker and weaker and was in pain everywhere.

Every joint and muscle let me know how much chaos they were in. I was stumped. This 'flu' really has me good this time. My husband rang at lunchtime, and he couldn't believe it either, as it was so out of character for me. I didn't know where to put myself, I was in pain, and I didn't want to take any medication to suppress the symptoms. I got desperate and took some pain relievers, and they didn't even work. Then I knew something was suspicious.

My mother wanted to take me to the doctor and I stubbornly refused, which is how I normally react. I will look after things as naturally as possible. I had chiropractic adjustments on Thursday and Friday, which usually aligns the spine so I can be in the best position for my immune system to fight whatever bug is in my system. But this time was different. My back was very stiff and so sore that I found it difficult to relax for the adjustment.

That night, I don't think I slept at all. Every single joint and muscle in my body was aching and screaming in pain. I couldn't get comfortable to save my life. I was moving and moving and I literally didn't know what to do with myself. My poor husband kept asking me if I was ok, and felt helpless.

SATURDAY, 3 AUGUST 2013

The next morning my mother put her foot down and rang the family GP who is a dear friend and chiropractor as well, who knows my personality and my values on health. I felt too weak to even go down the road to the diagnostic centre for a blood test. He ordered a nurse to come to the house. After he got the results he told my mother to take me to the Emergency Department immediately. I had no strength to argue, as I could barely stand at this point. I had no appetite, and I couldn't even stand in the shower.

Looking back, something told me to have Mark help me wash my hair and put in a braid, as I couldn't lift my arms above my head at this point. I was getting weaker and weaker. The blood test revealed my platelet count was extremely low. This was in fact nothing to do with the diagnosis I would get in the next couple of days. But luckily I was in the emergency room where medical emergencies are dealt with. It was so confronting for me. I pride myself on keeping a lifestyle that is based on health and wellness. That includes not taking drugs – pushed or prescribed. I had been exercising regularly and eating very well, which included a balanced wholefood (primarily vegetarian) diet.

I spent the night in the Emergency Department, very weak, very lethargic, yet still able to walk with assistance and still had my reflexes.

SUNDAY, 4 AUGUST 2013

What on earth was happening with my body? I felt more and more out of control. What was going on?

According to the Emergency Department, after an overnight stay of miserable tossing and turning all night and no answers, they couldn't find anything comprehensively wrong so were ready to discharge me that Sunday morning.

Still feeling like death, I tried to eat breakfast but was so weak I could barely get the horrible food to my mouth. I distinctly remember eating the prunes, as I was always conscious of having fibre in the diet, rather than the white processed bread they called toast, white processed cereal and processed sugar water, I mean juice. The hospital worker who served me said I was one of the only people he's ever seen actually eat the prunes. That was interesting.

There were so many overlapping symptoms, that there was no firm diagnosis. The doctors had concluded I could go home and rest, as it was just a 'bad case of the flu'. My husband, daughter and mother were there that morning to take me home.

In preparation to return home, I felt it was probably a good idea before we left the hospital to use the toilet. Still feeling extremely weak, I went to stand up and my abdomen was very extended from an extra full bladder. I didn't feel that I needed to relieve my bladder, so found this very alarming. All of a sudden, not even two seconds later, I was weeing all over the floor. I couldn't control my bladder and now it was wet where everyone had been standing as if an uncontrollable tap was on.

Nurses and orderlies were running to help and this got everyone's undivided attention. I'll never forget feeling and thinking, 'Red flag! Loss of bladder function!' Everyone was quite concerned now, including myself. Now they can narrow it down and firm up a diagnosis with this major symptom, I thought!

Nurses, doctors, specialists came in from all directions, asked me lots of questions; performed different orthopaedic and neurological tests to assess muscle weakness, reflexes.

At this point I could still wiggle my toes without any difficulty. The afternoon turned into an extensively long consultation while patiently waiting around the emergency department, observing many different people with many different problems.

The ER is nothing like the high action TV shows. There was a variety nonetheless. And I'm lying on the hospital bed, hoping that there's nothing overly contagious to contract while I'm playing the waiting game.

The hospital's neurologist was a very friendly young doctor. He treated me with an excellent bedside manner. While I'm thinking about the numerous possibilities that lie in front of me on the path that is about to unfold, I was understandably nervous, tired and anxious. My energy was slowly becoming more and more depleted as I'm wondering about all of the differential diagnoses that it could be.

I tried to remain calm and centred at the same time. I kept telling myself: 'I won't get anything that I can't handle'. 'What doesn't kill you makes you stronger'.

Honestly, I was still clinging onto a metaphorical cliff hoping that it was just a 'bad flu' – perhaps the worst flu of my life! The young neurologist asked me the question that I didn't hesitate in answering: "Do you want the good news or the bad news first?" He said it quite seriously but with a sincere smile. I actually didn't get to answer before he proceeded with, "The good news is that you will get better, but the bad news is that you will get worse before you get better…a lot worse…" "We are pretty confident that your symptoms are related to a condition called Guillain Barre Syndrome." The rest of his words were a blur as I then experienced the duality of shock and denial.

Ok, so I had something more solid to swallow here. I look at Mark, and look deep beyond his eyes into his soul. I know he is with me, not only physically, but on a soul level as well. I felt tears well up in my eyes as I remember studying this syndrome back in Chiropractic University 20 years ago!

I was taken back to the days when we studied Guillain Barre Syndrome and thinking to myself, literally, 'man, that would really suck.' GBS is described as a very rare, locked in syndrome where in the worst-case scenario you can die, or second best, all you can do is 'think and blink'.

Twenty years later, I ended up saying to myself: "Buckle up Pamela Anne, and get ready for the ride of your life!"

LOSING CONTROL

Another painstaking hour passed, and I was still able to wiggle my toes, but the reflexes in the lower limbs were completely absent. I was completely unable to walk now, unable to hold myself up standing; I couldn't do it no matter how much I tried. It was quite an awkward feeling, losing 'control' little by little, yet more and more over the past 48 hours. I wanted to run out of the hospital as thoughts of denial flooded my mind, 'This is not happening to me, it can't, I'm healthy and well, I've been doing the right things, it can't happen to me'!

"This is not about that". From the medical standpoint, there is no rhyme or reason as to who gets GBS, how old, how young, how fit or unfit...it's more of a random 'unlucky' event like winning the lotto (but like I said, unlucky, rather than lucky).

GBS – oh yes, can't move from the neck down... you can move

your eyeballs, and that's about it. WTF? OK, remember, you WILL get better. That's the HUGE difference here. You WILL get better. I reminded myself that the neurologist was pretty confident about that. He had no idea how bad it would get first, as it does affect everyone differently. However, I like to prepare for the worst and anything else becomes a bonus. So I was a little scared at first, but chose not to get too freaked out or anxious because that wasn't going to help anything. I looked at Mark as he stayed by my side while we waited and waited in the ER for further instructions from the medical team. My mantra was: 'This is not a permanent condition ~ *you will get better!'*

It's all about Perception at the end of the day. It's all about Mindset. I believe that to get through this, that is the #1 key. Most of the medical staff at the hospital later agreed that that was the main ingredient in my unsuspected 'speedy' recovery. Whilst it is a long process to regenerate nerves, I was able to bypass many days of self-pity and digression, rather than progression. I'll come back to this topic later…

After a few hours waiting for the medical staff to get organised, they came and told me that they felt it was best to put me in ICU in a private room straightaway so that they were prepared for however my body was going to proceed. It was still quite unknown over the next few hours. With the reflexes gone and severe weakness in my legs, I was however still able to wiggle my toes and I was quite proud of that. One of the doctors explained that there was the possibility of my lungs being affected so I may have to have a tracheotomy. He explained to me the procedure and whilst I insisted and actually believed that I wouldn't need that, in time that would all change. I admit I am a stubborn, determined and focused individual with a high pain threshold. However, GBS would challenge me like I've never been challenged before in my life.

INTENSIVE CARE UNIT

After wheeling me to my own private section of ICU, I remember being too weak to observe my surroundings in detail. Everything seemed to happen so quickly, yet take so long at the same time. Everyone was lovely, explaining what he or she was doing and asked me if I wanted a cup of tea.

I distinctly remember really craving a cup of nice black tea – no sugar or milk, just black. I never drink my coffee or tea hot; I am actually used to drinking it lukewarm, if not cold. When I was working as a chiropractor busy with patients it became normal to me. With all the hustle and bustle of the ICU Team in and out, asking me heaps of questions, I had to remind myself I am the patient here, not the doctor, unlike my own chiropractic clinic.

There would be 24/7 care with one-on-one nurse every single day and night, as long as I needed to be there. The denial kicked in. I won't need a tracheotomy; I just need some serious rest to recover. The medical staff were good in keeping the details to a minimum with me. They shared more with my family who needed to know those details for their own peace of mind.

Still wiggling my toes, smiling and chatting to the best of my ability, there was a lot to set up including taking vitals like blood pressure, temperature, and pulse rate. My poor family was getting tired of waiting around too and they were hungry. I had the cup of black tea next to me on the hospital patient table. I was getting too weak to reach it, yet too proud to ask for help. Each family member gave me a kiss goodbye and went to get something to eat, expecting to see me when they got back.

I didn't get to that cup of tea...

The last thing I remember was feeling weaker and weaker and extremely tired. I didn't get to see my family after they returned from their lunch.

My respiratory system was affected. My lungs were failing. The nerves were not communicating. The medical team declared this a medical emergency.

With that decision made, they put me in an induced coma; intubated me, stuck a tube down my throat and hooked me up to a ventilator so that my lungs could function. They put a catheter in place, a nasogastric tube, and hooked intravenous tubes up to me as if I were an alien in a pod from a movie.

My very last memory was when I was almost non-coherent and they allowed my family and closest friends to come and see me before I lost consciousness. It was as if I only had partial vision in my eyes as it drifted into a blur. My brother and his wife, Eric and Shannon, interrupted their holiday and flew home early just in case I didn't make it; if GBS stole my life; my parents, Ron and Ceci; my husband, Mark; my daughter, Marina; my dear friends, Lucy, Stacy & Byron. Everyone was very emotional, including myself, as their faces faded off into a hazy memory as they encouraged me with their unconditional love and support.

SURVIVED: ONE MILLIMETRE AT A TIME

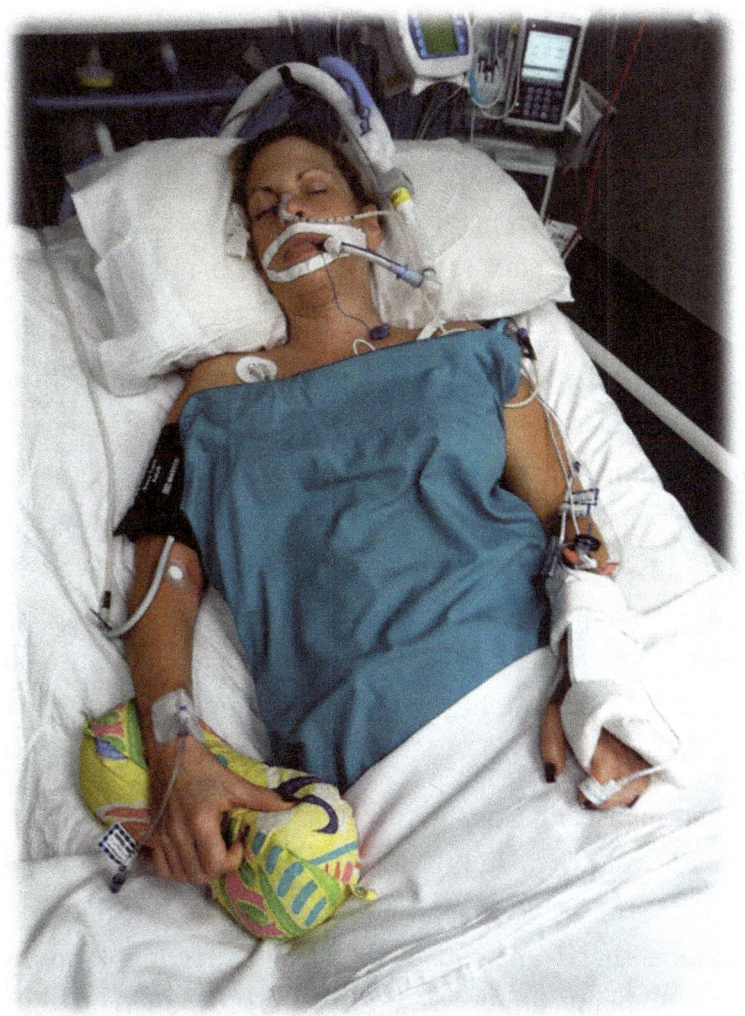

(Induced Coma - 5 August 2013)

AFTER THE COMA

I woke up a week later to learn I couldn't move – not one muscle. It was as if I was in a straightjacket. I was completely paralysed from the neck down. I couldn't wiggle my toes anymore, not even one bit. I couldn't move my head or my neck. I couldn't talk, which made communicating next to impossible. I was in immense pain. My neck felt broken and the headaches were terribly intense.

I had a very difficult time recalling what had happened since the last time I was conscious. I learned that I had been in an induced coma for about a week and my body had shut down fast...very fast. My surroundings were quite foggy; I was dazed and confused. I vaguely remember seeing a nurse and while she was asking me questions, I could not answer her. I felt helpless. I felt alone. I felt trapped. I felt isolated. I felt so out of control. This was the beginning of learning to let go...the true test of letting go...

I had so many emotions go through me. I was in denial back in the ER waiting to go into ICU. But there was no denial now. This was the real deal. Unable to move, I came to the realisation that I am *dependent* now - dependent on many people for many things. Now for an *independent* person, that was a tough one to swallow.

It felt as if GBS had dropped me to the bottom of the ocean, miles down into the dark abyss, as where Titanic lays to rest. I was alone, on the ocean floor, dark, cold, dead quiet and still. Unable to see anything around me, I knew I had to attempt to get to the surface. The only way to do that was hope that I would find some light to guide me. I imagined myself, ever so slowly, trying to find my way back. I just had to endure the time it took to get back to the surface. Whilst it wasn't easy, I reminded myself, it was possible. Keep the eyes on the light.

People would say to me, months later, 'Oh my God, I couldn't imagine'. That's exactly right, you can't imagine. I couldn't imagine it in my wildest dreams. This was no dream - this was my reality. Post-August 2013 will never be forgotten.

My life as I knew it would change forever.

"When all you can do is think and blink, you think...A LOT!"
~ Pamela Dunn

Chapter Two – I Am Not My Hair

"I am not this hair. I am not this skin. I am the soul that lives within."
~ Rumi

The morning before I went into the Emergency Department, I felt so weak that I could barely stand on my own. I could not shower myself and I really needed to wash my hair. I had Mark help me wash it and Marina put it in a braid to keep it out of my face. It was quite long at that time, half way down my back. I liked keeping it long because I felt it gave me a variety of options from leaving it down to putting it up, depending on my mood. I took a lot of pride in my hair and routinely had it cut, coloured, and treated over my whole adult life. I felt good when my hair looked good. I'm sure it cost a small fortune that would have added up, over the years.

The way I was feeling that morning, like '*death*' (I quote myself from a previous text message I sent friends at the time), I didn't care what it looked like, as long as it was clean and tidy.

During the week of my coma, there was a male nurse that sat

carefully braiding my hair while watching over me. This really had an impact on my family. I don't have that conscious memory. They told me this happened and that made me smile inside. The intentions were good, but the road ahead had other priorities in mind.

The nurses changed shifts daily and nightly, and understandably up- keeping the patient's hair was not high on the agenda. Life-threatening symptoms were monitored at all times, certainly not the state of my hair. I think it was washed once per week, if I was lucky, as that didn't fit in the 'vital' list of duties. I had a sponge bath daily, where they kept me relatively clean and fresh in the hospital bed. It was so laborious and time-consuming, that it was a treat when it actually was time for what they called a bath. The bath was more like a trough that caused more pain than what it was worth.

Anytime the orderlies had to turn me, they had to not only be mindful of the numerous tubes coming from the various parts of my body, but also had to gently hold my neck and head as well. My hair was not their priority. Luckily I could not see the back of my head and how badly matted it really was. The nurses and my family were able to give me the details while trying not to upset me too much. I tried so hard not to think about it.

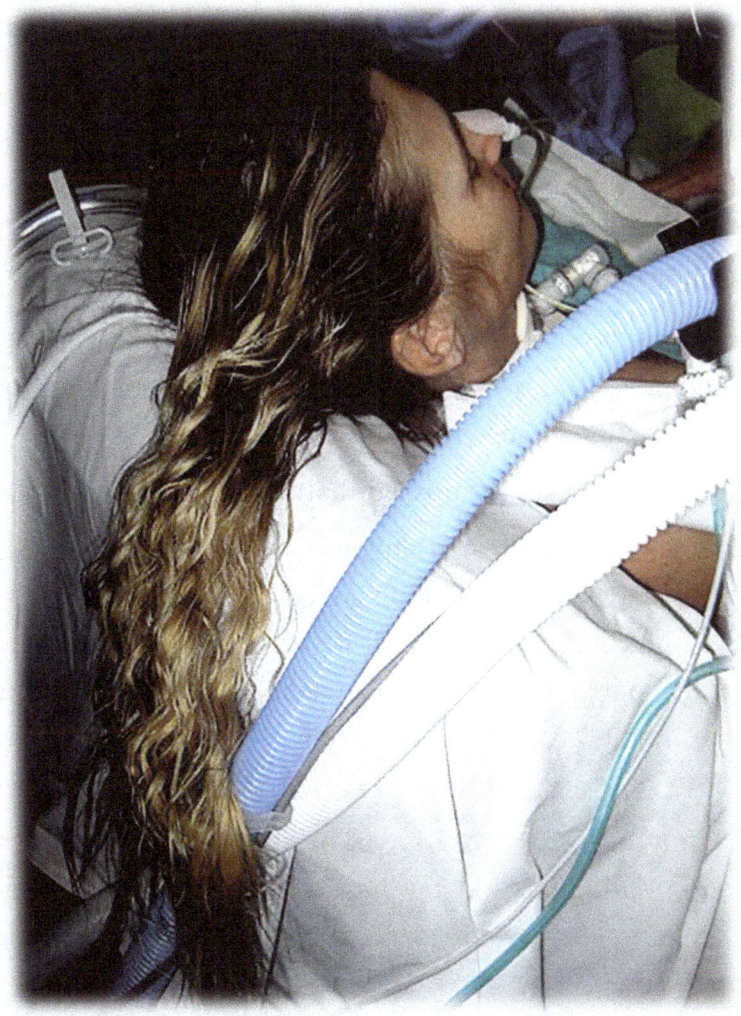

(August 2013 – early days in ICU)

THIS IS NOT ABOUT THAT

Through this process, I realised how important my hair had been to me.

It's easy to agree that our hair can depict how we feel. It's an extension of our personality. Hence the phrase, 'bad hair day' ~ our self-esteem can increase and decrease depending on how our hair is looking and feeling.

Hair is like an accessory that can be worn individually and uniquely. We tend to use our hair to express ourselves in any way we feel and choose, even if it's bald.

Just like jewellery, or tattoos, our hair creates personal style.

I don't think there's anything wrong with someone taking pride in their hair and making sure it's up to their standards. Healthy hair is beautiful and it can really transform the way you feel about yourself. Many people spend enormous amounts of time, money and energy in making sure their hair is looking good.

I certainly used to take a lot of pride and put a lot of care, attention and money in my hair with the salon treatments, cuts, colours, etc. I went to great lengths to manage my long hair.

Having a 'bad hair day' brings on a whole new meaning and if we really let it define our day, then a look at our priorities may just be in order.

THE HAIRCUT IN THE HOSPITAL

Having no control over my head, let alone my hair, there was a huge knotted mess of tangled hair that formed at the back of my head. I had one particular nurse, Melissa, spend almost 2 hours trying to get the knots out of the entangled disaster to no avail.

Rather than contributing to the potential dreadlocks, as this was simply not my style, my friend Stacy rang her hairdresser, Joanna, to come to the hospital and cut my hair. There was really no choice in the matter. It would make things easier not only for me, but for the medical staff in the hospital. It was a challenge that lasted 5 hours, yet in my vague memory it only felt like an hour. At that stage, I could not hold my head up on my own at all, not one little bit.

With that complication, it took a couple of people to hold my head up and as steady as possible, so that Joanna could get to do a decent haircut on me. I am so grateful for her time and effort.

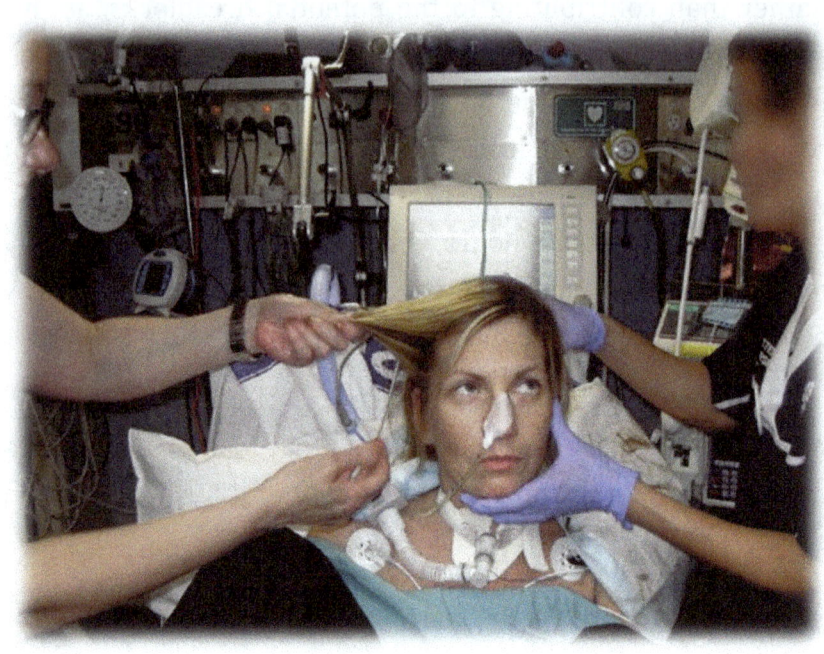

(The haircut)

I knew that it would be of no use over-thinking or worrying about it. Even so, I was so upset inside, but I also knew that there was a bigger picture. According to the way things were going physically, I wasn't going to magically get up from the bed and walk out of the ICU. The nerves needed time to regenerate. In the next week or two, no matter how positive I was, the facts are the facts. I was going to be lying in that bed for quite some time.

One to two days before the haircutting event took place, I went through a mental exercise of benefits and drawbacks to getting my hair chopped off. This included understanding that it will grow back, if I really want it to! It is not the end of the world.

"I am not my hair". I remember repeating this to myself in my head, over and over. That phrase didn't have a lot of meaning to me before. If you have a 'bad hair day' – it was like, 'Get over yourself'. I was actually faced with it in a totally different form; just to see how ridiculously unimportant it really is in the big scheme of things.

'I am not my hair' would have played and re-played over and over in my head morning, noon and night, whenever I didn't have my mind occupied with something else. I'm not ashamed or embarrassed to admit this because it is something that happened to me. I felt the relevance. I felt my acceptance and in the end, the practicality couldn't be overstated.

From memory I thought the 'big haircut' was about an hour.

Now, for a normal haircut, an hour is probably a little excessive. However, I later read in my journal and was reminded by Stacy and Joanna that it took them 5 hours to accomplish a hairstyle that would work for the rest of my time in ICU and into the recovery phase. Even though I couldn't feel it, I could feel it. Similar to when you normally get your hair done, it just felt better after. A fresher aspect and mentally knowing that I wouldn't have dreadlocks now, I felt better within myself.

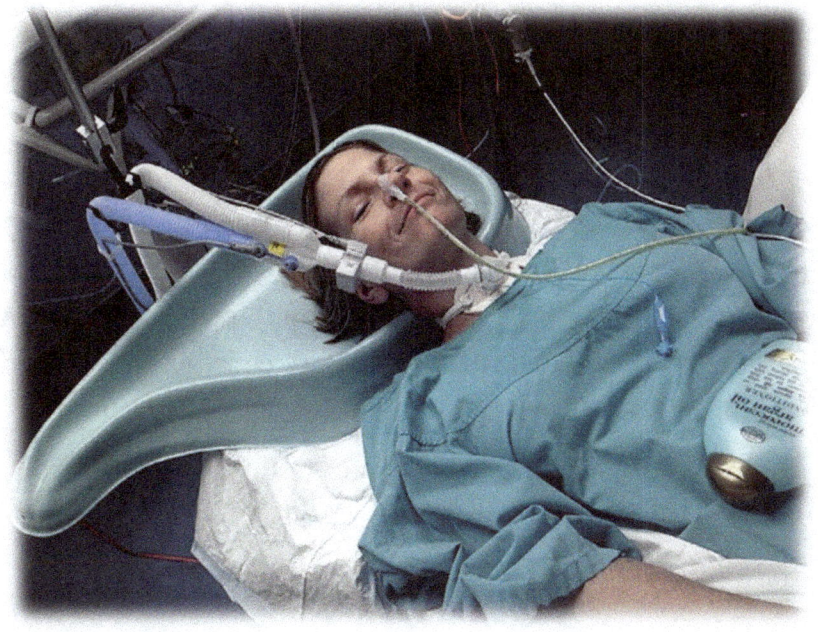

(Hair washing in ICU)

When I was able to move my head more myself, as I grew stronger, it was so much easier for the nurses to look after it. Then in Rehab, when I was with physios every day doing exercises to strengthen and awaken my muscles, I could push it back with a headband and off I went...in the wheelchair to the next appointment!

When I was out of the critical stages and even out of rehab, it was still quite difficult to do anything with my hair. Due to both of my shoulders being frozen, I couldn't raise my arms to wash and condition my hair, let alone style it! This slowly improved (and I mean slowly) to the point where each week I would monitor my progress by what and how I could groom myself. This included how much help I needed in the shower, washing my face, brushing my teeth, putting makeup on, etc.

DETACHMENT

From:

Our egos

Our looks

Perfectionism

How we see ourselves

How we perceive others see us

Routines

Things out of our control

These are some of the thoughts that went on in my head, in the early days of ICU:

Does my hair make me a better person? Does my hair define me? From my experience I can say, with certainty, that hair should neither define nor consume an individual. To some reading this, it would be obvious and to others, it may cause you to think about your own feelings if you were faced with the situation.

I have a new sense of admiration for people that have lost their hair due to illnesses such as cancer. There are numerous people that have to deal with this all of the time. I reminded myself that 'it could always be worse' and that I wasn't losing all of my hair. It was just much shorter than I would have chosen at the time.

So it was really about choices. I didn't make the choice to have it chopped off, and I felt 'out of control' in the situation.

Is my hair more important than my blood pressure being regulated? No. Is my hair more important than my breathing capacity? No.

Is my hair more important than the other bodily functions that I couldn't control? No.

Is my hair more important than the nasogastric tube that was providing my system with nutrition? No.

Perspective. Put it all into perspective.

BALANCE IS RESTORED

This situation brought a lot of issues to light. This really wasn't about 'hair'. This was the beginning of ditching the perfectionism and becoming more authentic – comfortable, real and raw. No perfect hair, no makeup, and no style in the clothing and shoe department. Hospital gowns are not exactly attractive.

I was faced with a choice ~ a choice to get upset, angry, resentful at the situation. Or accept it, embrace it, and let it go. This was my opportunity to look inside and see beyond 'the hair'.

When I was finally able to return home from the rehabilitation hospital and able to walk (very slowly with splints), it was time to go to the hairdresser and have a proper cut and touch up from 3 months of hair neglect.

Stacy took me back to see Joanna. She was so gracious in coming to the ICU to cut my hair in the early stages when I was barely conscious. She was so pleased to see me recovering and able to hold my head up, to sit and walk slowly. She chuckled to herself, as the hair in the back of my head wasn't as uneven as she thought it would be due to the degree of difficulty in the hospital.

She gave me a neat trim to even out my hair and some foil highlights to freshen it up. I admit it felt so amazing after all of those months of 'bad hair days'. This time it truly was a treat.

I remember the sun was shining and on the way home Stacy and I stopped at a local café for a coffee and sat outside enjoying the beautiful day. Balance was restored.

THREE YEARS LATER

Just over three years later, my hair was at the length that it was when I went into the hospital in August 2013. After some personal reflection, I decided I was ready to 'cut it off' again, but this time it was **my choice**. The opportunity was there and I went with it. I did this for me, and only me.

I'll never forget, my long-time friend and hairdresser Brenda asked me if I was sure. And when I looked at her and spoke with conviction, she knew it was more than 'about my hair'.... This was a personal thing, and I was doing this as part of my soul healing.

Now I totally embrace it. I love it. It's the 'new me' from a looks perspective. I also decided not to fully colour it anymore. I will only have foils to highlight and keep some natural colour coming through. It was the perfect opportunity to change the hairstyle. We can really get attached to insignificant things like that. Or should I say significant?

Our hair should not be the major deciding factor on how we see ourselves, or how others perceive us. Our hair is definitely a part of us, but it's not all of us. After all, at the end of the day...*it's just hair.*

Chapter Three – The Pain

"Your pain is an opportunity for you to learn about yourself."
~ Gary Zukav

I got confirmation from my family that this warrants a chapter for itself. I don't believe that it is spoken about, nor addressed, nearly enough. If it happens to you or a loved one, then knowing the possibility of this severity is very important.

THE BACKGROUND

Before my experience with GBS, I would say I had a pretty high pain threshold. It started from a very young age that I can remember.

For example, when I was a small child, my mother was advised to take me for the allergy testing with all the needles in the back and in the forearms. This was no fun time. I was very unimpressed with feeling like a human porcupine. Then I went on to have the anti-allergy treatment that entailed numerous needles in the arms. I believe that this period of time was the start of when I learned and developed how to disassociate from pain and what was happening to my body.

Another memory of pain disassociation was when I fell backwards from an aboveground pool ledge onto the ground and broke my left arm when I was about 5 years old. This was my first plaster cast experience. I was at a neighbour's house, feeling fearless and invincible as kids do. I wanted to show my mother how I could dive into the pool. As I turned to tell her to watch me, I lost my balance and fell outside the pool, instead of into the water. I quickly learned that those ledges were not for standing and jumping from.

Another example from when I was a child; I split my chin open in the second grade, running in gym class. I was paired up with the fastest boy in the class, and being the competitive person that I am, I did my absolute best to keep up with him. Being only 7 years old, I wanted to win, but tripped on the shiny floor right onto my chin. I recall having a white shirt on and I kept assuring everyone, including myself, that I was 'fine' and tried to brush it off, until the blood was all over my sleeve from rubbing my chin. I needed 7 stitches. It wasn't just a bruise that I could brush off. My mother was horrified when she came to pick me up from the school office to take me to the doctor for stitches.

About a year later, it was Easter Sunday. We had a large Pontiac 1977 Grandville, which in those days had extremely heavy doors. My brother was trying to be a gentleman and close the door for me when I got in. Unfortunately, while he was trying to do the right thing and impress my parents, he slammed the door on my leg (by accident). My mother told me to get out of the car and I tried and tried to walk on it and shake it off. I managed to fight back the tears and 'be strong'. Hours later we found out it was actually broken. This was my first experience on crutches and yet another plaster cast.

Fast forward to seventh grade, I was outside on the playground during lunch recess with friends. We were being kids, and rolling and balancing a huge, heavy telephone pole that served as a border in the parking lot. In one of the rolls, my foot got caught under the pole which rolled backwards on it, causing significant damage to my right big toe. I managed to walk back to the class when recess was over. As we were reading in class, I noticed my right foot, primarily the big toe, throbbing in pain. I took my shoe off and the white sock was now red at the forefoot and full of blood. It ended up that it was broken and the entire nail came off and had been removed from the weight of the telephone pole reversing over my foot. No tears.

One more example, which is simply to give the background of the pain threshold, was having my daughter naturally without any prescription drug intervention. No doctors, no hospital, no gas, no epidural. Hours later, my healthy baby girl was born weighing 8 pounds 6 ounces with the assistance of some brilliant midwives in a birthing centre.

When I was in my 30s, I had a good healthy habit of coming home between shifts in my chiropractic practice, and doing water exercise in the pool in my backyard. One day, rushing around to get back to the office on time, I went to shut the door to the storage closet outside and got my little toe (same right foot) stuck in the door as it slammed. It was extremely painful. I was home alone, could barely walk so I crawled into the house, up the steps to get dressed again for work and dragged myself into the office to see patients that afternoon. It was broken, but with toes, there's not much you can do except let them heal on their own. Nerves of steel at the time, I saw my patients that afternoon and smiled the entire time. I would not let that foot get me down. After all, that's why we have two, isn't it?!

So I'd say I handle pain pretty well. My experiences contributed to my pain threshold overall.

DESCRIBING THE PAIN

GBS gave me the test of my life. No one could have told me or prepared me for what I was about to endure.

When I was diagnosed in the Emergency Room before they transferred me to ICU, I had to mentally prepare myself for the road ahead of paralysation. My logical brain knew that I was going to be unable to move, but I had no idea what it really meant. How is anyone adequately prepared? And it happened so quickly!

Here's a brief anatomy and physiology overview: the myelin sheaths are the protective coating of the nerves. The nerves are stripped of this protective coating extremely quickly, and left 'raw'. Not only was I unable to move, I was also extremely hypersensitive - I could feel sensations, in a very, very bad way.

If someone was touching my feet with pressure of 1 out of 10, it actually felt like 20 out of 10 to me.

When someone asks me what the pain was like, this is what I say:

"Imagine your whole body getting hit by a huge 18-wheeler truck. Then imagine that truck reversing and running over your body again. Next, your body gets doused with Napalm, set on fire and run back over with the 18-wheeler truck again."

That about sums it up.

Am I exaggerating? No, not at all. Then imagine being stuck like that for weeks and weeks and unable to tell anyone...because you can't speak. The body also felt after all that torture, that the bones were broken and hypersensitive, as if dragged over hot coals. I swear if I didn't know any better, that my neck was broken too with the headaches and neck pain that I woke up to.

There is no magic pill or magic drugs for the pain that can be endured with GBS. There was a specialised group of doctors at the hospital that were designated as the 'Pain Team'. They would come into my room on average once per week and see if my pain was getting any better. I would signal with my eyes 'NO!' and they would assess and change medications accordingly. What I learned was that it was a lot of trial and error. Virtually every 24 hours that passed was a hope that the pain would subside.

What I also came to realise was that the medications only barely took the edge off it. If it was 20 out of 10, getting it down to 11 out of 10 on the pain scale was winning. I was in pain the entire time that I was conscious in the ICU. Everything was extremely hypersensitive and there wasn't a thing I could do about it.

It took all I had to accept the amount of medication that I was intravenously prescribed. It bothered me so much, knowing what was being pumped into me. With my health background, I avoided medication at all costs. In those early days of ICU, Mark did some research on the side effects that all of the drugs could cause and in turn tried to get me to battle the GBS on my own. He called me the 'Queen of Pain' from my past pain threshold, and then asked me 'where she was'. I was so angry inside I thought I was going to kill him. In hindsight, it was good that I could not move. I could not scream. This was the hugest form of implosion. The unknown and unpreparedness of this health crisis was nothing short of overwhelming. I would have chosen to have 10 babies naturally in a row, than to go through this.

The equilibrating fact here was that western medical intervention was essential in this medical emergency. Without it, I would not have even had a chance to survive, and I am grateful for it. I came to accept that once I was out of the critical stages of GBS, I would look at measures to rid myself of the toxicity that would be running through my body.

MOVING POSITIONS

Every position that the patient needs to be moved into can cause significant pain and irritation. This needs to be considered for the patient, and the medical staff that are looking after the patient need to take extra special care.

In ICU, they had to periodically weigh me as part of the medical protocol. As I could not stand on a scale, there was a huge contraption that would serve as a body sling and they could weigh my body. I felt like a huge rotisserie chicken. It was one memory I would be happy to forget. Unbelievable: completely dead weight, hospital gown all open in the back, going up like a prize chicken to weigh in a human deli. This was not only a bit humiliating, but painful! Each strap was pushing on nerves that were raw and unhappy. However, this was something that was unavoidable and unfortunately necessary.

Another position move that was very tricky was the 2-hour turnover every single solitary day. Every 2 hours, there was a team of four orderlies that came to assist the movement of the patient's body from side to back to the other side and back again. This was repeated every single day, and through the night it was every 4 hours from memory. They did their best to be gentle and efficient, especially as I was conscious when it was happening. Most people in ICU are in a coma and unconscious.

The pillow was crucially important to support the neck properly. As a chiropractor, I always slept with a supportive pillow. Mark brought in my latex contoured pillow so that my neck was supported not only on my back but also on my sides, to minimise the wrong curvature in the neck. This is something that I would highly recommend for patients going through this or in a similar situation.

Another extremely painful positioning move that caused me great anxiety was when they had to take a chest x-ray while I was in the hospital bed. Moving my body in a very abnormal position while getting the hard cassette behind my back while I couldn't support myself caused immense pain, and I couldn't speak to tell them that. That is another memory I'd like to forget.

And one last one: the daily hoist that was similar to the chicken weighing apparatus, to move me from the bed to a chair. This was to get the muscles moving in a different position to just lying on a bed in the horizontal position. I dreaded it like the plague. I really hated the daily sitting routine, as my neck was 100% unable to hold the head, therefore sitting exacerbated the pain. It was part of protocol and I understand why, but that doesn't mean I liked it.

A-HA MOMENT

That's when I decided that if I was going to make it through this horrific scenario, then I was going to change my focus; I would have to address something else. The mind. The mind is a very powerful thing. This was my opportunity to call on all of the personal growth and development tools that I have invested in and learned over numerous years.

DR PAMELA DUNN

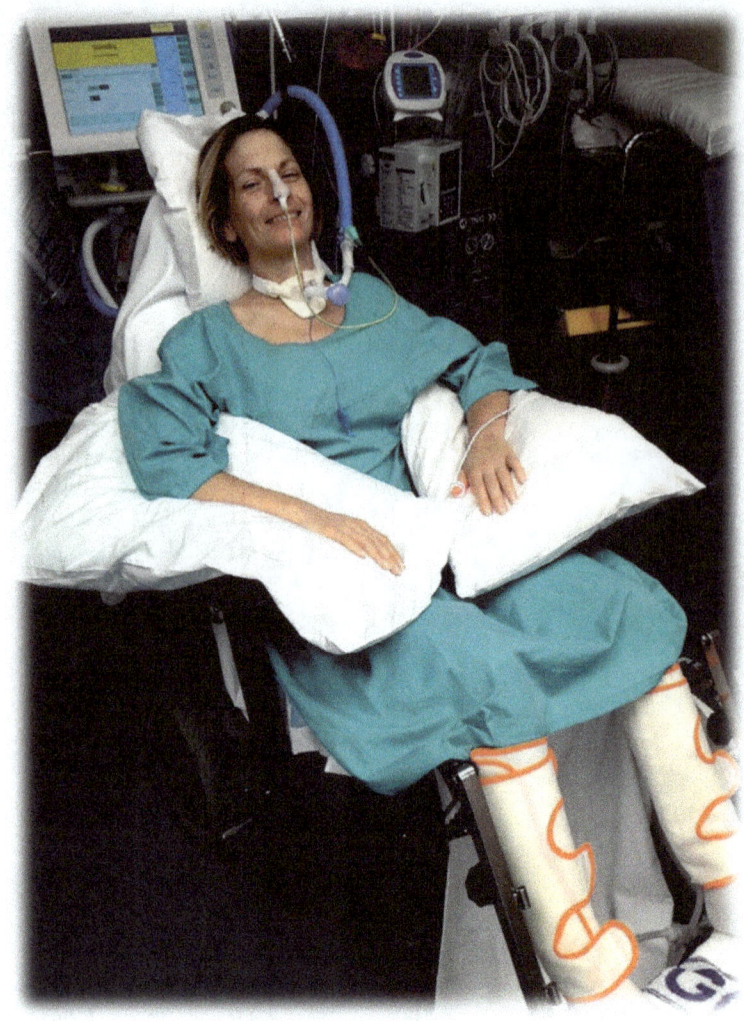

(Smiling keeps the spirit alive)

I still had a choice. I could choose to feel like a victim and be angry, upset, resentful and frustrated. Or I could choose to look at the other side. In other words, there is a reason for this, and trust that it will all be revealed, in time. I decided then and there that I was going to be a survivor. My mindset was surviving, getting through it, as I believe we are not given anything that we can't handle.

Chapter Four – Letting Go

"Let go of the attachment to what was, and look forward to what may be; what is right now and what is really important..."

~ Pamela Dunn

"The art of letting go is simply about personal empowerment. Realising what you're in charge of, realising what you control, and more importantly what you don't control."

~ Steve Maraboli

This may just be the most important chapter of this book. To me, I believe that 'letting go' is one of my biggest lessons. If it weren't for the GBS journey, I would not have learned what I needed to learn the most. Pretty significant, when you look at the extreme severity of it all, but I accept the responsibility and hold accountability of the manifestation of this life lesson that started approximately 5 years ago.

OUT OF CONTROL

When is enough *enough*? On the outside, I appeared to have it all. I was a successful chiropractor with 2 practices, a loved daughter, sister, mother, wife, friend, and colleague to other health professionals. I enjoyed my life, tried to see the bright sides of things, the glass half full; I was the eternal optimist. I lived by the beach, close to my practice, close to my parents and had a network of friends not only in Australia but in other countries as well, especially the United States.

I did have some internal struggles, perhaps due to being in my early 40s and in a sort of mid-life crisis wondering about the true meaning of life. Was I living life 'on purpose'? Was I on the right path, and which direction should I take moving forward?

I felt like life was moving so fast. I felt rushed. I would think these things, but not really reflect. There's a difference. Thinking without turning your brain off is different to being still and reflecting, allowing ideas and even solutions to flow. I didn't feel like I had a lot of time to breathe. Sure I was breathing, but not really *breathing*.

I felt as if I was driving on the freeway of life – speeding, in fact. One of my friends used to joke and nickname me 'Lotus Esprit' after the sports car, reminding me to change gears once in awhile instead of virtually driving on high speed all of the time. I laughed, but deep down I knew he was right. Feeling like I had no real choices, I kept up my busy, fast-paced life and tried to make the absolute most of it.

And in just a split second, in the blink of an eye, it was as if there was a brick wall in front of me. No avoiding it. I hit the wall with full impact. It was like a head-on collision.

In hindsight, it was more like a freight train at full speed crashing into a wall with no warning, and with no control of the direction.

My brick wall was the 'significant emotional event' – SEE – that would change the rest of my life forever. Not a severe car accident, not cancer, not a death, nor a traumatic world event. For me, it was GBS. It forced me, without will, to give up control, to surrender, to let go, of E V E R Y T H I N G.

Letting go can feel like losing control; but this is a perception. Shift the perception and realise it is not losing control. It's not about what happens to you; it's about how you respond. And how you respond determines how you survive it. That is the true key.

The learning goes in stages:

ACCEPT

TRUST

SURRENDER

LET GO

MANIFESTING OUR REALITY

About 12 months before I was diagnosed with GBS, I was on the most amazing cruise in the Caribbean having the time of my life, listening to three world renowned speakers, wining and dining, dancing and planning my future. I would say that that trip was one of the highlights of my life – a definite pinnacle in my timeline.

Creating a 'vision board' was one exercise that we did toward the end of our 2-week cruise on one of the largest ships of the world at that time, The Oasis of the Seas.

We spent a good couple of hours contemplating and cutting out inspiring words and pictures from magazines, while having quiet reflection time. Funnily enough, the main theme for me that took up the most room at the top centre of my board read, "Learning to Let Go". At the time, I was simply inspired by the words. Who knew what was in store only 13 months later.

BE CAREFUL WHAT YOU WISH FOR

Letting Go had new purpose in my life. "Ask and you shall receive".

Well, I asked, and now I will receive. I had no idea at the time what was in store for me. Thoughts are so powerful. Trust me. I thought that it meant reading another book or two and using the power of the mind to just 'let go'.

At the start of the cruise in June 2012, I made a conscious decision to learn how to meditate. The power of manifestation was in full force.

This led me to my roommate on the ship being a person from Perth who taught meditation! That was amazing in itself, and to this day she is one of my best friends.

Well, perhaps that was just the beginning of the path that I decided to take. 'Learning to Let Go' was my theme in many aspects, with the climax being GBS. It takes enormous courage and strength to go through these terrific challenges that come across our paths.

Twelve months after the cruise, July 2013, I was feeling quite exhausted physically, emotionally and mentally, and in desperate need of taking a break. However, I couldn't see an easy way to do that. I felt I had the responsibilities to my patients in my chiropractic practice, financial responsibilities, parenting and other family responsibilities, etc. When you think you have no choice, think again.

As I was getting ready for work one day that July, I said these exact words to Mark:

"I'd give anything to take 6-12 months off…."

He just looked at me. Two to three weeks later, I found myself in Sir Charles Gairdner Hospital awaiting the dreaded diagnosis. Things happened so quickly, and it wasn't until later that I realised the significance of that statement I had made. That is how powerful the manifestation process can be.

I look back now, and although I can't turn my life back to that time, I am continually sharing with other people to listen to their bodies; pay attention to the signs if you need to make a change in your life. Whichever of the seven areas of life it's in – vocational, familial, financial, physical, mental, spiritual or social – have the awareness to recognise it and find the courage to make the change. Make a move in a relationship, career, geography, etc. Don't wait or there may be something that will push you there that you can't even dream of.

Recognise your soul screaming, or it will scream even louder until you make the change.

IT'S A CONTINUAL PROCESS

I must admit, I was quite naïve back in July 2012 when I did that vision board and decided to do a few meditation classes to think I would get the whole process of 'letting go' and my life would change…quickly.

Due to my naivety, my soul had an interesting and quite intriguing way to get me to truly understand and evolve on a slow, steady path of spiritual growth. After all, it's what I 'wished for'. I wanted to be more spiritually evolved with a change of consciousness.

Nearly 5 years later, as I write this, I am faced with the realisation that it is a process. Letting Go is a process like the layers of an onion. I always think of the movie 'Shrek' here. It's not just turning a light-switch on or off. There are many layers to peel on the journey and after you get through one layer of the onion, there is another one to get through. After that onion layer, there is another one, until you have peeled the whole onion, metaphorically, or 'mastered' the lesson.

Another movie that comes to mind is 'Groundhog Day'. We can choose to live Groundhog Day the same, over and over and over. But if we pay attention, then we can make changes to make 'today' better than yesterday, if we are mindful and make adjustments and improvements to the way we handled 'yesterday'.

We can choose to see monotony in daily life, reliving the same patterns day in and day out; or we can see it as a brilliant opportunity to improve on the last. As another day closes, what choice will you make? This is what I asked myself every day, and continue to do so to this day.

I'm not perfect, and continue to have different struggles always presenting themselves. I can have good intentions, but unfortunately don't do everything that I want to implement regularly every single day. It's a work in progress. I am on a continual journey of trying to improve that. However, I do know that by implementing strategies one step at a time, one bite at a time, one day at a time, when you look back, you realise how far you've actually travelled, and how much you actually have achieved.

How do you eat an elephant? One bite at a time. How do you eat a frog? One bite at a time.

Rather than staring at the overwhelming mountain in front of you, take it in baby steps. Another valuable lesson for me: GBS recovery was literally 1 millimetre at a time; one small step at a time - figuratively and realistically.

And anything worth anything takes time. Time. Timing. Patience.

PATIENCE

Patience is another skill that I needed to learn and develop to survive the GBS experience. Patience not only for myself as the patient, but for the family and friends support network. This cannot be overstated. It was a lesson in patience for all involved.

The layers of the onion in regards to developing patience started with the acute stages of ICU when I could literally do nothing but 'think and blink'. No moving, no eating, no walking, no talking, no drinking. That was the biggest layer. I had to rely on everyone for everything.

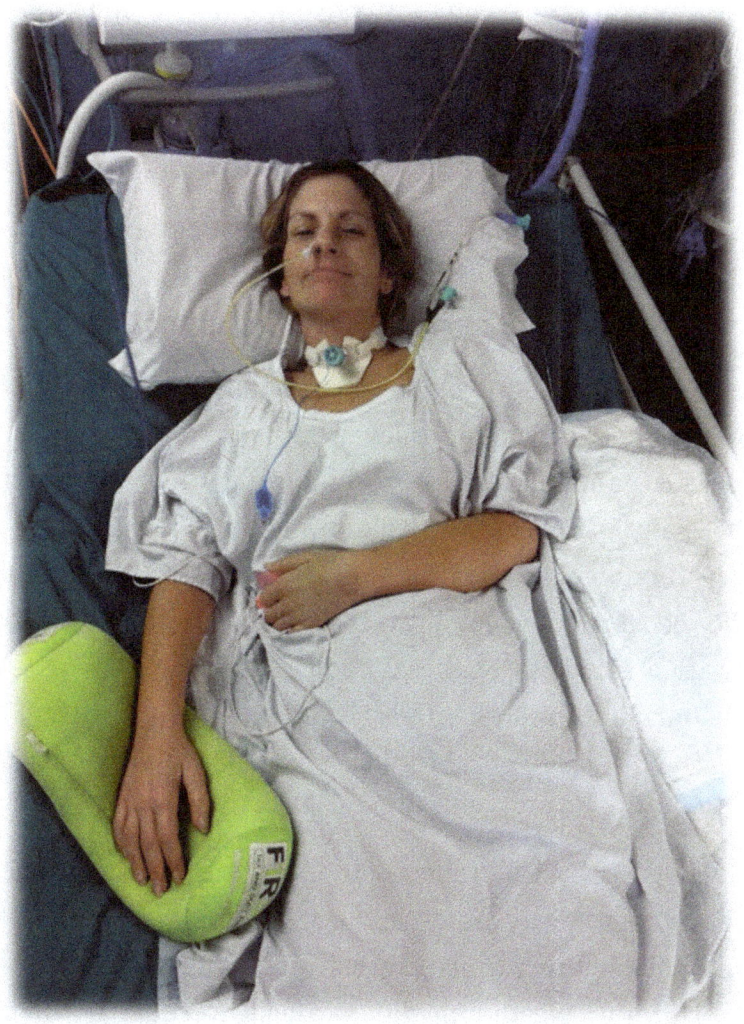

(Learning to Breathe in ICU)

The next layer was on the recovery being so slow. Learning to breathe on my own again took weeks of rehabilitation. Patience.

The next layer after that was learning to sit on the edge of a physiotherapy plinth for 10 seconds. Patience.

The next layer after that was learning to stand – assisted. The next layer was standing – unassisted. The next layer was learning to feed myself. And this went on and on. Patience.

When I returned home from the hospital after being an inpatient at Rehab, there was another layer of the onion to get through; or was it another complete onion? I came home in a wheelchair, as I could not walk on my own yet. I also had two frozen shoulders as the ranges of motion were nowhere near in the recovery stage yet. I was basically a skeleton of skin and bones that could only talk, eat and get up from the wheelchair for a short few minutes with assistance. It was a long way from the early ICU days, yet a long way to go still. More layers – more lessons.

Besides the physical rehabilitation side of things to teach patience, there were other lessons in letting go. Things that would have bothered me before, like an untidy house, dust on the furniture, weeds in the garden, were now virtually unimportant in the big picture of things. They would get done, but after the priority issues were done. This was another onion that had many layers. I told myself that it would get done in time, and to focus on what was more important. Sitting in a chair waiting for someone to bring me either a drink or something to eat was how it was for a while, and another reason for me to work hard in rehab to get better and gain my independence once again.

I did my very best to be a 'patient' patient. Mark was my main carer and he did virtually everything when I came home. Cooking, cleaning, wheeling me around in my wheelchair, taking me to the toilet numerous times throughout the day and through the night, helping me in the shower so that I wouldn't fall over, driving me to appointments almost every day and doing household chores like grocery shopping, laundry, etc. My daughter helped out as much as she could and I am so grateful for their patient natures as it was challenging to say the least. I did my best to not be demanding and reminded myself how lucky I was to be home now and getting better and stronger every day.

MY LIFE IS FOREVER CHANGED

Now, I would say my developed sense of patience serves me well. It has been a lesson that has strengthened different areas of my life that weren't there before.

Another huge lesson in letting go for me was with my career. I decided when I was 9 years old to be a chiropractor. I had complete focus and determination to become a chiropractor and help others as it helped me as a child. When I had to face the reality that I may never practice again, it was as if someone ripped my heart out of my chest. My hands were my life. I thought that at the time. It was something that I just had to trust: that there was a bigger picture here.

Whilst I have my life back, it is different. I was so busy with my chiropractic practices before GBS. On one hand, that was a good thing. Being successful, but at what cost? I felt that I didn't have time for certain things because I was 'too busy' with running the practice, seeing patients, running errands, doing family things, socialising, packing it all in.

I had to 'let go' of all of that. I remember distinctly feeling all of the energetic cords releasing so that I could get back to a state of balance. I loved being a chiropractor, and I loved my patients, but at the end of the day, I had to change that focus and focus on my health and my recovery ahead.

This was a golden opportunity to re-set myself, like re-booting a computer, trusting there was a bigger picture, and all would be revealed, in time.

I also had to 'let go' of the life as I knew it from a financial perspective. I distinctly remember lying there in the early stages, only able to think and blink, and realised that if I had all of the money in the world, it wouldn't even matter. Money can't buy health, it can't turn back the clock, and it can't get me better any faster. This was a massive lesson, and realisation. Knowing it is one thing, but experiencing it is another. I got the message.

I used to be quite stuck on some poor financial decisions that were made in the past; decisions that I thought were mistakes and never really got over. As I had the time to reflect on this in the hospital, I was able to forgive myself for the past and change my mindset. My outlook has changed, and whilst money is important, health is number one. Without health, you literally have nothing. This was an opportunity to re-set my mindset around money and find a healthier balance that will serve me better.

Chapter Five – The Power of the Mind

"The length of time it takes for you to recognise your outer crisis as a blessing correlates with your degree of wisdom. Pure wisdom is the instantaneous knowing that each crisis in life is indeed a blessing. Some misfortunes don't reveal their blessing easily, while others are recognised immediately. Hidden within all misfortunes are the seeds of an equal but opposite fortune.

You won't be confronted with a crisis you can't handle."
~ Dr John Demartini

THE GREATEST ASSET

My mindset would have been my greatest asset in surviving GBS. My family and close friends agreed. The medical team at the hospital also agreed.

There were numerous times throughout my life before GBS where I was accused of living more 'in my head' with overthinking, not trusting and not feeling. I had worked on this over the years through personal and professional development. Being 'in my head' ended up having new meaning and my developed and adapted version served me well here in this situation.

When I was first admitted to ICU, and the diagnosis was made, the head doctor took Mark and my parents aside to let them know that there was a very rough journey ahead. Because of the severity of my case of GBS, and the extent of how my body was affected, (as in the need for life support; complete paralysis; motor loss; and sensory deprivation), they had to give a prognosis.

The hospital doctors on staff tried to prepare my husband and family so that they could receive emotional support, and encouraged psychological counselling for all immediate family members including my then 16 year- old daughter. I was admitted early August 2013, and they told my family to prepare for me to be there in ICU, hooked up to life support through Christmas and that I could be in that state in ICU well into the next year.

When Mark heard this, he refused to believe it. He knew that if I had the right headspace, and that my needs were being met the best possible way, by all involved externally to myself, that I would be recovering and home much sooner than that.

A prognosis is really only a 'guess-timate' based on other people, and other information that is similar to, but certainly not the same as each unique situation.

When I heard this, my inner dialogue with myself was something like this:

"Hell No! You will be out of here sooner than that; as soon as you feel any remote sense of even a little spark of nerve communication coming back, you will be working as hard as you've ever known to work to recover. It's Showtime Pamela Anne! You got this."

The doctors probably thought I was a little bit delusional back then, knowing what they knew in regards to the condition. However, they would have been basing it on their past experiences with GBS patients. They didn't know me at all: my background, my personality, my values, my strengths, my weaknesses, my support network (family and friends) and what I was capable of. I felt that I had the ability to tackle this with as much conviction, focus, determination and strong will that I could tap into. Being a competitive and stubborn individual would actually work in my favour here.

The mind is the most powerful thing. If we can overcome the obstacles in the mind, the body follows.

"You have power over your mind – not outside events. Realise this and you will find strength."
~ Marcus Aurelius

BELIEF

Whilst the mind is powerful, belief is essential. Truly believing that I would get better, from the deepest parts of my soul was the difference – not just thinking it.

- Belief in Self.
- Belief in My Support Network.
- Belief in the Medical Team.

I've never been in a more vulnerable position - completely dependent on absolutely everyone. This was about getting comfortable being uncomfortable. If I 'thought about it' too much, that would have been detrimental. I hung onto the belief that 'all of my needs are met' and belief in all those around me to do their best in my care.

Believe that 'THIS TOO SHALL PASS'. Believe in this. It will pass. It will get better. I will improve. Albeit slowly. Each week was better than the last. Believe it will get better. I kept affirming the above, day after day, night after night.

FAITH

Take that a step further. Belief is a product of the mind. Faith is a product of the spirit.

This was the greatest challenge of my life. I knew that deep down this was happening for a reason, and trusted that all would be revealed in time.

It gives new meaning to 'keeping the faith' when you are presented with a great challenge in life. I had faith that 'this too shall pass" and allowed myself to 'feel' it deep within my soul. I did not abandon God or the Universe, nor did I feel abandoned. I felt great love, on a spiritual level, like I've never known before.

"Real faith is not a statement of beliefs, but a state of being. It is living life mid-air — standing commando on a tightrope fifty stories up with no preconception of the outcome. It is trusting beyond all reason and evidence that you have not been abandoned."
~ Rea Nolan Martin

FOCUS

Focus needed to change. Focus needed to be directed where it would be productive and serve on the road to recovery.

This was not the time to be 'present'. Normally, that's an ideal way to live. I do my best to do that on a regular basis. Not stuck in the past, or worried about the future. I feel that Life is a balancing act, and if we can use our wisdom that we gained from our own past experiences, learning and growth, that our future will present with opportunities and experiences that we may not even imagine.

That's not to say that we shouldn't plan or have goals, but one of my biggest learnings is that being 'resilient' is the key. How resilient you are is how well you actually respond to situations you are presented with. Not just reacting out of guilt or fear, which are emotions, but how well you are able to 'weather the storm'. I have learned that if you're too attached to an outcome, then the pain of the lesson can be even greater and more difficult.

Life is like the weather. There will be sunny days, rainy days, cloudy days, and stormy days. If they are all the same, that makes life boring and uninteresting. So some of the 'inclement' weather days are necessary to really appreciate those sunny and more pleasant days. Funnily enough, that's why I love living in Perth so much, because of the sunny days making up the majority of our weather.

RESILIENCY

How resilient you are will determine how well you tackle life's challenges that are thrown at you. GBS was my test of tests. I knew that. I felt it, literally in my bones. I knew that I had two choices. My choices were: deal with this the easy way or the hard way. The hard way was remaining angry, upset, resentful and frustrated. The easy way was believing with conviction that 'This too shall pass."

I believed and had unwavering faith that there was a 'light at the end of the tunnel'. I literally made a decision that I would focus on the teeniest pinpoint of light at the very long tunnel ahead of me. I did not want to focus on my situation that kept me paralysed 24/7 in the ICU bed, hooked up to numerous tubes and machines that made me feel like an alien in a pod that was in a straightjacket. I did not want to know what it looked like, or what the room looked like around me. I only relied on what I could see in front of me when I looked around forward and peripherally. Because I couldn't move my head, I couldn't see the full 360 degrees. I was mentally ok with this, because I actually didn't want to.

To this day, I still don't know what the room actually looked like, except from my view from the bed looking in the one direction. The room was in the middle of a floor in the hospital. There was a door and a window that looked out into the hall of the hospital ward, so there was no window looking outside. It was so bizarre to have everything so regulated that you literally lost track of time. Time had a new meaning. I had no way of knowing what time it was, day or night, except for the clock that stared at me every single solitary day on the top of the wall in front of me. Eventually someone put a calendar on that wall with a countdown of days that I was in there, as I lost the concept of time, not only daily, but the days that folded into weeks.

THE LIGHT AT THE END OF THE TUNNEL

So back to that pinpoint of light at the end of the tunnel: the facts remain that I was determined to get better. I wanted to get better. Not one day went by that I didn't keep my eye on the light at the end of the tunnel.

After waking up from the coma, realising I wasn't dead, that I didn't pass on to the 'next place', wherever that may be, I knew without a shadow of a doubt that it wasn't my time. I then consciously decided that I had a lot of work to do, and I still wanted to be here on this earth for the human experience.

I can understand that not all people would feel this way, nor would they choose it. Everyone is entitled to his or her own prerogative. I honestly felt that I was too young and had way too many reasons not to leave the earth yet. Only the individual can answer that sort of question for themselves when faced with the dilemma.

I also know that I wasn't afraid to die. It's a huge statement, I know. I can honestly confirm that for myself. Fear did not come into the equation at that time. I came so close to the end, and felt unafraid. When that choice is presented to you, it's amazing what goes through your mind. If I didn't wake up, then it would have been ok with me too. I had a sense of inner peace that I would be ok. I just wanted to make sure that my family and friends knew that I loved them, as I didn't have an opportunity to say good-bye.

I made the conscious decision every day to keep laser-focused on that pinpoint of light at the end of the tunnel. I knew in my mind, (even though I may not have felt that way physically every day, due to the pain and associated difficulties), that I would be that little millimetre closer, each and every day.

*(The light at the end of the tunnel –
I took this photo 2 weeks before my GBS diagnosis)*

HEART

I'm not talking about the cardiovascular system here. I am talking about the heart linking to the soul. Having a 'why' to get better and get my health back on track. Having a true 'why' made the crucial difference. I wanted to get better. I felt I had so much more life to live. I wanted to see my daughter grow up. She was only 16 at the time, still in high school with the rest of her life ahead of her. I saw not only flashes of my life, but her life that I would love to witness. I wanted to be a grandmother one day. There were so many places in the world that I hadn't been to yet, and I've always loved to travel. There would be so many unforeseen experiences to share with my husband, family and friends.

The burning in my heart was so strong for my life; the life that I cherished and appreciated more than ever. This fuelled my desire to fight to live, to go the distance, to endure the hardship ahead of me. I knew it would be tough, but I also believed with every inch of my soul that it would be worth it.

The heart-mind-body-soul connection really transformed during the whole process for me, and continues to do so. The amount of tears that came during the writing of this book, re-living the events, the emotions, the 'movements of my soul' was astounding.

I am more in touch with my heart and soul after the GBS journey than I ever have been. I used to be a much more body and mind type person. To experience true unconditional love is the greatest gift in the world. Without it, you have nothing.

LOVE

Love's definition, as quoted by one of my greatest mentors: Dr John Demartini:

"Love is the synthesis and synchronicity of complementary opposites."

I stuck to the belief and knowing that love is all there is, and all else is illusion. My state was temporary, as I kept reminding myself over and over and over in my head. 'It could always be worse', I would remind myself day after day, and continue to do so.

I felt love energetically like I've never known before. I knew people loved me, but I really felt it immensely – not only from my family and close friends, but also from every one that I was connected to, in one form or another. I felt the love, the prayers, and the blessings. It was one of the biggest gifts of my GBS experience.

Truly feeling and being in touch with the energy, was contributing to the development of my inner feminine. I am eternally grateful for the unconditional love that I received from my family and friends, and never feeling alone. There wasn't one day that went by in my entire hospital stay that I didn't have a family member come and visit me.

Even though I couldn't communicate one word, I did my best to 'speak' with my eyes. And if you can tune into that, then you really understand when people say 'the eyes are the windows to the soul'. There was always someone there at my time of need, during the painstaking days and nights. I never felt alone.

IMAGINATION

When I was physically alone, especially during the night and naptime during the day, I took myself on inner journeys. When I didn't want to think about the situation or the next procedure one of the ICU staff came in to implement or record, I went 'travelling' in my mind.

I accessed the best, most vivid memories I could recall and went as deep as I could, as if I was there. I went through the list in my head of my best travelling experiences, the best vacations, things that made me smile internally and things that moved my soul.

For me, some of the places I re-lived in my mind were trips to Disney World in Florida; the Caribbean Cruise; Mexico; Hawaii; and childhood trips across the United States.

I also called in my deceased grandparents, as I see them as angels. I had soul-to-soul conversations with them quite regularly. They continued to give me guidance and assurance on a soul level.

This key activity helped to keep my own sanity when I had the time on my own. I found it so helpful in my recovery that I make it a point now, in my current life, to not only continue to make magic memories with different experiences, but really tune in and consciously make the effort to imprint them in my mind.

For example, when I go on a holiday, I will consciously and intentionally take in the surroundings and fill all of my senses - with not only what I can see, but what I can hear, what I can smell and, when the food is memorable, what I can taste with every taste bud on my tongue.

It's more than just 'having the experience' – it's being intentional to be 'present' and then committing it to memory.

Since the GBS experience, I have been on some very memorable holidays that I cherish beyond belief. I look at the pictures I took on my camera relatively regularly to remind myself of the wonderful times. I replay the highlights over and over in my mind, especially during different forms of meditation. I would highly recommend this whether there is a tragedy or not. It was an excellent tool that I felt played a key role in my recovery. It's something that no one can take away from you - a part of you that only you know, as your experience is yours and yours alone.

Investing in experiences and memories is what I continue to do, to contribute to part of a fulfilled life. This doesn't have to include indulgent expensive holidays, although they are always lovely. They can be memories from simpler experiences such as:

- Being in nature, appreciating natural beauty – walking, hiking, cycling
- Having a lovely cup of tea or cappuccino by the beach
- Watching a magnificent sunset with a glass of wine
- Conversations with friends with no time-restraints
- Relaxing by a fire, with a good book
- Observing different areas of your own city that you have never been to
- Going to a live music concert or play

As long as they are in alignment with your own personal values, then those memories will serve well.

Chapter Six – Memories of ICU

"He who has faith has an inward reservoir of courage, hope, confidence, calmness, and assuring trust that all will come out well - even though to the world it may appear to come out most badly."
~ B C Forbes

THE COMA

You would think that you wouldn't remember anything. In my mind, so much was revealed to me on a subconscious level while I was unconscious. This was quite interesting, reflecting back, as there were significant issues going on in my life, which lead to bouts of uncertainty. And with that uncertainty came fear of the unknown.

For me, the week that I was in a coma lead to so many valuable insights that I consciously replayed them over and over in my head, so I wouldn't forget as I couldn't speak them nor write them down. I did not want to forget the incredible details and the messages that came with the visions, dreams and hallucinations that I had.

There was no concept of time. I had no idea I was in a coma until

I woke up and everyone told me I had been in one. That was such a bizarre feeling. For all I knew, it could have been a day, a week, a month or even a year. I had absolutely no idea.

It gave me focus too. Focus to keep my mind active on something that I wanted to remember. The time I had day after day, allowed me to process properly, without being rushed, and without the regular distractions of daily life that can get in the way.

MY NEAR DEATH EXPERIENCE

My 'near death experience' was the true moment that changed my life forever. I thought I was dead, yet I wasn't sure. I found myself in a blacker than black box – black ceiling, black floor, black walls with no light whatsoever. I didn't really know if I was dead, because I pictured 'dying' differently.

Thoughts went through my head: What would it be like to transition to that next place? Would I be greeted with angels with big wings and flowing white gowns? Would I be walking on clouds? Would it be so bright and beautiful that I would be speechless? The answer was No. My experience was nothing like that.

My conversation between God and the Universe went like this:

"Am I dead? I must admit, I'm a bit surprised as I'm only 43 years old... but if I am, it's ok. I'm not afraid. I just really hope that all of my family and friends and people whose lives were connected to mine in one form or another know that I love and appreciate them...and if I'm not dead, and I wake up from this weird black box, then I know I have A LOT of work to do..."

And not long after that, I woke up. There were no voices back to me. No bright lights, just an inner knowing that it wasn't my time.

> *"Do not let what you cannot do interfere with what you can do."*
> *~ John Wooden*

BEING CONSCIOUS IN ICU

There is a very good reason why the Intensive Care Unit (ICU) is called Intensive. Twenty-four hours a day of monitoring the patient. Vital signs and statistics are constantly and continuously monitored and recorded. When I was there, unable to move, I was able to observe this work in detail.

I admit I really had no experience or knowledge in this department before. I avoided hospitals like the plague, and besides my grandparents having hospital stays that I recall when I was a child, I only really went to the hospital to visit a friend having a newborn baby.

It was almost humorous, as I learned that a lot of nurses in ICU are not used to interacting with conscious patients. With a little chuckle to myself, as laughter is a form of healing in itself, I tried to make light of the situation. Most patients in ICU are unconscious, so the nurses' duties are to record their vital statistics, keep them clean and make sure there are no emergencies and if there are, then know how to deal with them.

Yet there were some nurses who were like angels and I made a conscious decision to focus on them, the positive ones. They would try to make conversation with me, and not only look into my eyes, but connect on a deeper level. This was an opportunity to really appreciate the human experience and give life deeper meaning.

In my case, I was conscious unless I was sleeping. I couldn't communicate with my mouth, but I did with my eyes. I was aware of my condition and I was able to observe all that went on around me. I did my best to be a 'patient' patient, and as compliant as possible. It was so difficult being on the 'receiving' end, as I was used to 'giving' all of the time in my own practices.

In the early days, I experienced some grand hallucinations that had me wondering what was real and what was not. They brought up some deep issues that I had been struggling with emotionally and obviously hadn't dealt with completely. It's important to deal with our 'demons' or they lurk in the background until we do. It gave me some real insight into what I needed to work on from a personal and professional level.

I also was able to dial into people's energy, more than ever. When one or more senses are taken away, the others become stronger. This was definitely the case for me. I didn't have to spend any time eating or drinking, or going to the bathroom. There were no mundane chores, tasks, lists that take up so much time in daily life. I was able to stop and literally **really stop**: no moving, no talking, nothing. I could only see with my eyes and hear with my ears. I don't recall smelling much either which is probably a blessing in disguise.

I chose not to have a television, as I didn't want the distraction. I didn't watch it at home, and I didn't want to watch it in there. I preferred music, but not the genres that I would normally listen to. Mark organised various CDs with healing music that I believe were much more beneficial.

Mark also purchased a crystal Carillon Bowl that focused on vibrational healing. Between him and my friend Stacy, they came in and played it almost every day for me.

CORDS AND TUBES

There were so many cords and tubes to keep me alive that it was astonishing.

It made it even more difficult to move me, as the patient, due to taking extreme care of all of these tubes hooking me up to different machines. I felt like a weird alien creature in a movie where they have all sorts of cords coming out of their body. Without these numerous tubes and devices, I wouldn't have had a chance to survive. This was a medical emergency, and I believe western medical intervention was crucial.

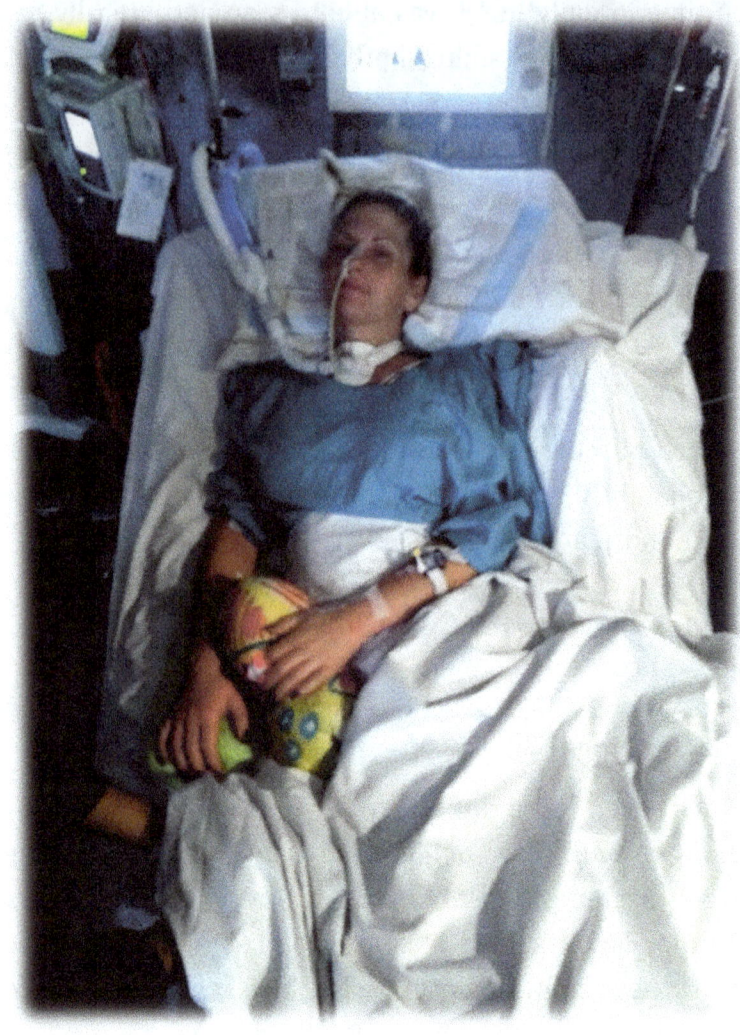

(A normal day on the ventilator in ICU)

I remember the days felt like being in a constant straightjacket, unable to move at all, not even wiggle. I felt like someone had buried me in the sand at the beach, and all that was sticking out was my head. So no matter how hard I tried to move a hand, arm, foot, leg, etc. it was impossible. It was the strangest feeling; I just couldn't move. I felt completely disconnected from my body.

The trach tube was hooked up to a ventilator after the tracheotomy was performed. The tracheotomy was a surgical procedure, consisting of an incision to the trachea (windpipe) that assisted my lungs in breathing as they had failed due to GBS. When I was diagnosed, the doctors said my case was in the severe category. It was so severe that it affected my lungs as well as my motor functions; plus I ended up with pneumonia as a complication as well.

Suctioning happened several times throughout the days, performed by either the nurses on duty or a respiratory physiotherapist. The purpose of suctioning is to clear mucus from the trach tube so that the air is unobstructed and as clean as possible.

The nasogastric tube was inserted from the nose down to the stomach to keep me nourished. This was there for about 10 weeks. I was unable to eat anything or drink anything on my own, due to not being able to swallow my own food. Not one drop of water, not one bite of food. The blessing was that I could honestly say that I was never hungry, nor did I crave anything.

The catheter was inserted through the urethra to drain urine from the bladder. The defecation process happened involuntarily and unbeknownst to me. This would be discovered at various times of the 2-4 hour intervals of changing positions.

The PICC line (peripherally inserted central catheter) was inserted into my arm primarily to save the veins from numerous needles. This was used for blood tests to monitor the blood and for IV (intravenous) medications.

It was kind of like being an adult baby - completely helpless and reliant on everyone for everything. Everything was done for me, from being sponge- bathed to having clothes changed (lovely hospital gown), to being fed (through the nasogastric tube), to the comfort (relative) of temperature and mattress.

My heart and associated cardiopulmonary statistics, including blood pressure, were constantly monitored. This was actually so insightful during the beginning stages for me. Unless you have been diagnosed with a heart problem or lung problem, chances are you don't realise how miraculously that system works in your body. I knew how it worked, physiologically, but did I *really* appreciate it?

There were also the white anti-embolism socks that had to be worn 24 hours per day and a contraption fitted to the lower legs that helped with the circulation by lightly squeezing in and out, compressing the calves. I remember being able to feel that compression movement on my legs before I went into the coma, and yet unable to for the rest of my stay in ICU. I dreaded having the nurses put them on. It was like putting tights that are too tight on a child that doesn't cooperate - very difficult and actually painful.

Let's not forget the orthopaedic boots that must be worn to prevent and (hopefully) avoid foot drop in order to recover properly. They were big and bulky, similar to the moon boot that one needs to wear for a fracture in the foot. They had to be worn the vast majority of the time during the day and night and this kept the foot and ankle at 90 degrees at all times. As much as I resisted silently inside, as they were so uncomfortable, I came to realise the great importance of them afterwards and during my rehabilitation phase. Without that continuous support, the chances of foot drop increases dramatically. There is also risk of abnormal function of the Achilles tendon and calf muscles.

There were so many beeps and sounds of the equipment not only in my room, but also in the hall and fainter sounds from other rooms' equipment. This would normally drive me crazy, but I learned rather quickly to tune them out, or it would literally have driven me nuts.

INSIGHT – DOCTOR NOW THE PATIENT

Let me explain the confrontational scenario here. I am a philosophically based chiropractor who highly values health and wellness. I choose to deal with health and medical issues as naturally as possible. I have always chosen to live by the motto, 'Chiropractic First. Medicine Second. Surgery Last'.

When there is little to no obstruction, the body is fully capable of healing itself. I believe this with 100% of my being. However, when the body is under stress – emotional, mental and/or physical - this compromises the body's healing ability. The body ends up in some form of 'dis-ease' where there is chaos instead of order.

The tables were now turned. I was so used to being the doctor in my own practices, being the leader, and assisting people on their road to health as a chiropractor. A lot of this was educating people not only about their health and how to look after it, but about their bodies internally and how they worked.

Now it was my turn. There I was, lying in the bed, completely helpless, and dependent on absolutely everyone else. This was quite an adaptation for me as a fiercely independent woman!

In the first week or two, I was very frustrated as you can only imagine. So many unknowns, so many things I couldn't say or do, and not knowing what on earth to think or feel. Pre-GBS my resting blood pressure was always in the normal range, and if anything it would tend to be lower and never high.

There were a few significant incidences that happened in the early stages of my time in ICU that caused me a great deal of aggravation. I got so incredibly frustrated inside, that my blood pressure went so high it caused alarms on the machine. Remember that I could not speak, nor voice these frustrations. The adrenaline that would have been pumping through me would have been like a pressure cooker.

Nurses came running to see what the matter was, and after that happened a couple more times, I realised I needed to get on top of this. I thought to myself at the time: my emotions are getting out of control; I am allowing this to happen. I am responsible for this, and the aggravations are not going to contribute to my health getting better. I decided to be accountable and responsible for my actions and more importantly, for my reactions to events 'out of my control'.

Although I was 'out of control' physically from the paralysation perspective, I could still control my mind and my reactions. No need to play the victim here. That would only impede my recovery.

In normal life, how many times do we do this on a daily or weekly basis? Making the heart and circulatory system work in overdrive to deal with the challenges that are thrown at us. How much adrenaline is pumping unnecessarily, leading to more stress and health-related issues? I reflected on this numerous times after my hospital experience and even years later into my recovery. We don't really get to feel and understand how much our physical bodies are affected by our emotions and the way the body has to work to continually balance the physiology.

COMMUNICATION

Lack of Communication is more appropriate here. Communication had new meaning. Try to lie perfectly still and not say one word for an hour. You could probably do that during an hour meditation class. Multiply that by 24 hours and multiply that by 8 weeks. That's a lot of time to not be able to move or communicate.

The 'locked in' aspect of GBS came to fruition when I felt so trapped inside myself. I would hope and pray that people could read me and try to figure out how I was feeling and what I wanted or needed.

The lack of communication tools available is astonishing for GBS patients, and somehow people just get through it. I had the use of my eyes for blinking 'yes' or 'no' and I tried so hard to move my mouth so that someone could *try* to lip-read. I thought I was moving my mouth, but on the other end, no one could really make sense of my very limited lip movement. This contributed to a massive amount of frustration in the early days. You're never really prepared for it, and there is a huge learning curve.

Looking at a board with letters to spell words would take

forever, so only the basics were covered. It was too time-consuming and frustrating. The lack of verbal communication for me was probably more difficult to get through than the physical paralysation itself.

My immediate family did their best to try and figure out how I was doing on a daily basis in relation to pain and discomfort. I was also very fortunate to have a dear friend who was able to really dial in and connect with me on a different level. Her name is Esmat, and she was like an angel. With her background in massage therapy, she used her knowledge and skills to assist in reducing the pain and problems associated with lying paralysed day in and day out. Knowing my body from previous muscle work before GBS, she was able to massage the areas that needed it most. The most severe area on the day dictated where she focused her hands. Some days it was my neck, other days it was my feet; and other days it was my trunk where the breathing muscles were affected. The lymphatic system was severely compromised during the whole hospital stay and she worked in assisting the lymphatic drainage as well. I believe that this area is quite overlooked and now with my first-hand experience, I would encourage others to look into this area for patients in the same or similar situation.

Taking away the communication aspect from the equation gave me the opportunity to focus more on other aspects of the whole situation. I was also able to really learn and appreciate other professions through the GBS experience. As a chiropractor in a private practice, I did not have hospital experience, or involvement with intensive care or even rehabilitation facilities that are in hospitals. I knew of it, but actually experiencing it is priceless and invaluable, especially for me as a health practitioner.

The learning and appreciation I have now is remarkable. There were some very special people that worked in ICU when I was there. I'm not sure if I was just extremely fortunate, or if that's the case everywhere. I'd just like to acknowledge the team at Sir Charles Gairdner Hospital, Perth during the months of August and September 2013 for not only the medical care they gave me, but for their individual spirits that touched me deeply on an energetic level in the big picture of things.

A special mention and huge heartfelt thank you to the:

Orderlies/HSA – for the endless turns in the hospital bed, day and night, while making sure my neck was in the right position on the pillow, and that all the tubes and cords were unobstructed - smiling and having senses of humour I will never forget.

Respiratory Physiotherapists – the crucial care and importance of the lungs and breathing physiology, the suctioning (salty water).

Occupational Therapists – the patience and care for the minute details of the beginning stages of hand and arm rehab.

Rehabilitative Physiotherapists – the patience and care during the early stages of larger muscle and nerve rehab.

Nurses – dealing with me as a conscious patient in ICU; doing the best they could to keep me comfortable.

Specialists – the individual attention and care.

UNCONDITIONAL LOVE

As horrific as the situation was, the love I felt lying in that hospital bed, day in and day out, from the selfless attention of my family members: my husband Mark, my daughter Marina, my mum Ceci and my dad Ron, my brother Eric and his wife Shannon, was invaluable.

I was also able to feel the love and prayers from all of those connected to me, near and far. The generous gifts and cards with the most beautiful words of encouragement made me smile inside and out. It helped to continue bringing the whole scenario into balance.

Everyone felt quite helpless, as there wasn't much they could do in the beginning. There were so many unknowns. But for me, lying there, I was just happy that they took the time out of their days to come and see me, and be with me. It's the little things that count at the end of the day. Just a warm smile, a kiss on my forehead, brushing my teeth and washing my face with a warm flannel was like heaven. They went out of their way to make sure that my needs and wants were tended to the best they could, and I couldn't be more grateful.

At the end of the day, love is all there is, all else is illusion. Relationships and the experiences that you can treasure make quite an impact and leave lasting imprints in your memory.

> *"I've learned that people will forget what you said, people will forget what you did, but people will never forget how you made them feel."*
> *~ Maya Angelou*

SMALL MIRACLES

Before I was admitted to the hospital, I had tickets to George Benson and tickets to 'Michael Jackson the Immortal World Tour by Cirque du Soleil' – a tribute to the music of Michael Jackson. I was so upset and disappointed that I would miss these events due to the timing of GBS. The George Benson concert was in the first few weeks of me being on life support, but the Cirque du Soleil show was about 8 weeks later.

I did miss the George Benson concert. Mark and our friends stopped into the hospital first to visit me, and then went on and tried to enjoy themselves.

Now I had a new goal: Cirque du Soleil! If my body was the least bit able to attend, then I would do whatever I had to do to get to this show. The combination of Cirque du Soleil and Michael Jackson were forms of two of my very favourite entertainment. Besides recovering to the very best of my body's ability, I wanted to see the world with new bigger and brighter eyes, and I wanted to experience things like never before.

As I did show signs of improvement with minor hand movements and lungs being able to breathe on their own, I worked as hard as I could to improve make it further still. This was very difficult and draining, but I felt like a military general was in my head to train me while using every bit of strength I could muster.

I asked the doctor if there was any way I could go to this event, at all. It's so crazy looking back, I can't believe it happened. It was so surreal. He said, "I won't say yes, but I won't say no either."

That's all I needed to hear. A couple weeks later, after the intense respiratory physiotherapy, I was able to breathe on my own long enough to be escorted by ambulance to the Perth Arena to see the show. I was in a wheelchair, still with the nasogastric tube and in immense pain, but I enjoyed the show so much with my friends, my husband, my daughter and the doctor and nurse who came with us.

(Perth Arena – awaiting the show)

It was surreal. I rode in the ambulance, lying on a stretcher. As I was still unable to sit unsupported, I was then transferred to a wheelchair right outside the front of Perth Arena. I'll never forget how beautiful everything appeared. The evening sky was like velvet with stars shining bright like diamonds. The fresh crisp air was tantalising, and I couldn't believe I was finally outside the walls I had grown accustomed to in my ICU room. The murmurs of people walking to their seats awaiting the start of the show filled my ears. It was alive! It was a glimpse of feeling human again. The show was spectacular. At the end, I was escorted back to the hospital via ambulance and from the sheer excitement came the deep exhaustion. I crashed into a deep sleep, which my body craved after such an event.

This was the beginning of the end of my days in ICU.

Chapter Seven - Memories of Rehabilitation

"Sometimes it takes dealing with a disability - the trauma, the re-learning, the months of rehabilitation therapy - to uncover our true abilities and how we can put them to work for us in ways we may have never imagined."

~ Tammy Duckworth

So much was packed into this phase of my GBS recovery. I have noted only the highlights and the things that impacted me the most. The Rehabilitation Phase of my GBS Recovery consisted of 1 week's transition in the Neurological Ward of Sir Charles Gairdner Hospital, and 3 weeks at Shenton Park Rehabilitation of Royal Perth Hospital.

TRANSFER TO THE NEUROLOGICAL WARD

The day in ICU finally came when I had learned to breathe on my own, and was no longer reliant on the machine that provided life support. What a huge accomplishment and the beginning of feeling true freedom. After numerous hours that were spread out over weeks of respiratory physiotherapy, and the regenerating nerves that were supplying the lungs recovering, I was discharged from the ICU to the Neurological (Neuro) Ward of the hospital. Depending on how soon I progressed and if a bed was available, I would then transfer to Shenton Park, Rehabilitation Centre as an inpatient.

I had very mixed feelings with the transfer from ICU to the Rehabilitation Phase. I found this very interesting, as I reflected back. As happy as I was to leave the ICU, because that meant I was progressing and getting better, there were mixed emotions of sadness, fear and anxiety. I was sad because all of the people that were looking after me for the last 2 months would probably never cross my path again. I had a hard time digesting this fact. I was scared and anxious because of the unknown. I had actually become 'comfortable'. By being 'comfortable' in the situation, was the classic sign that it was time to move on – move on to the next phase in my recovery.

This ended up being only a week in the Neuro Ward. I started with Occupational Therapy where they fit braces for my hands and wrists, to help the contractures and muscles heal. I also started a more intensive round of Physical Therapy where I started my Milestone List.

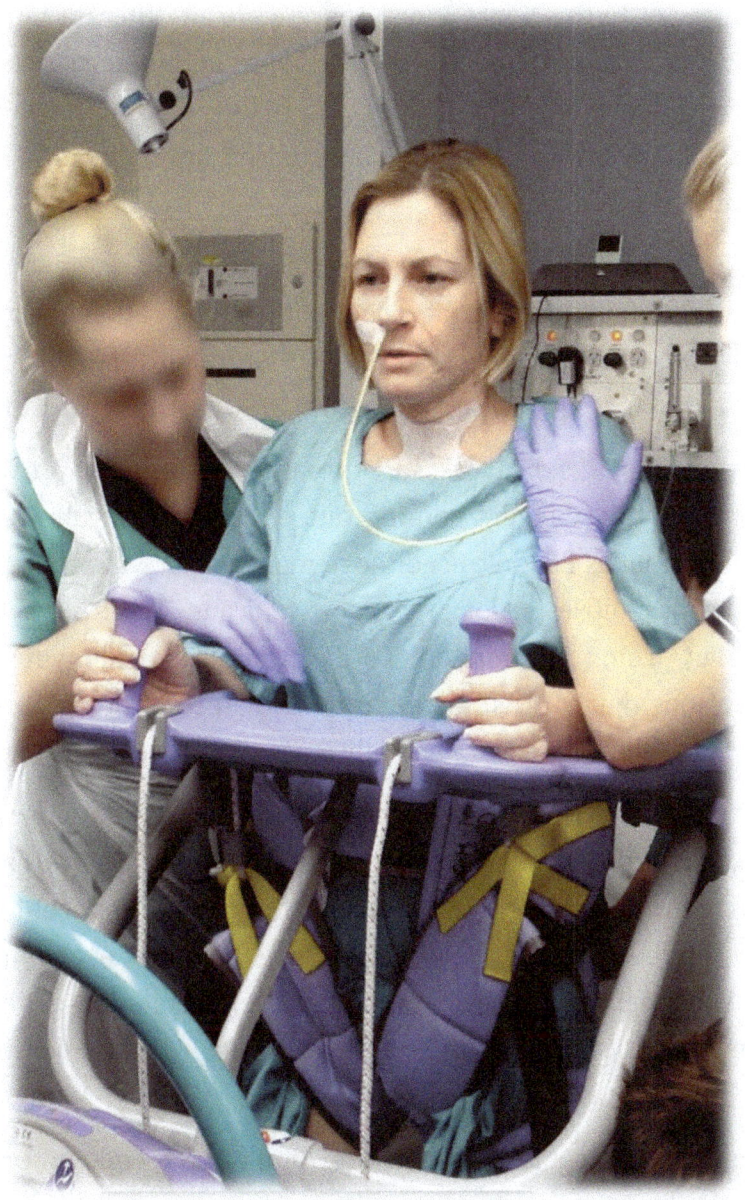

(Learning to stand again)

When I got to the Neuro Ward, there were all different nurses, and their compassion levels were quite different to what I had got accustomed to. Unfortunately for me, the nurses had quite a few other patients that needed attending to, and I wasn't 'special' anymore.

I had to learn how to eat straightaway, if I wanted to get rid of the nasogastric tube. I couldn't wait to get that thing out of my nose. I already went through the dreadful blister stage and dry skin on my nose in ICU from the tape that held it there.

My throat felt like the worst sore throat of my life; as if there were 5 million tiny daggers coming out each time I swallowed. I realised that as I hadn't used those muscles for 2 months, they would be a little out of practice. It took me about a week to recover from the horrible sore throat issue, allowing the adhesions that formed inside to heal. Instead of being excited about eating again, it was actually a very painful experience.

The incentive to get the throat used to swallowing and progressing from mashed food to real food was the threat of them putting the nasogastric tube back in. Not a chance! I was determined to get better every single day with every single meal, no matter what. The digestive system needed to get back to normal, slowly but surely, and that was a whole re-learning experience as well.

The catheter came out but if I didn't pass enough urine, which they measured, then they were coming back in with the catheter to extract more urine from the bladder. I dreaded this and have tried my best to get rid of that painful memory.

The constipation that resulted from no physical movement for 2 months and the cumulative side effects from the prescription drugs that I was taking was horrendous. That is another extremely painful memory I would love to forget. Let's just say that there's a lot to be said for getting enough fibre in the diet combined with the right amount of movement.

We don't always think about these things, until something happens and we are forced to face it. The bodily functions that I had taken for granted had to be re-learned, one little bit at a time. I appreciate my body more than ever for those autonomic nervous system functions that we don't have to think about...until we have to think about them.

The first 'real food' outside of hospital food that I wanted was pizza. Once I could really appreciate the taste and was able to swallow half-decently, I enjoyed a slice with friends who came to visit. It was a very special moment.

I also remember the ceiling hoist, which was so cumbersome yet necessary to move me from the bed to the wheelchair to the toilet or shower. This was another lesson in patience. Once I could do these things with assistance, it meant I could sit on my own (over the toilet or in the shower) for a short time. This was a sign of progress. I was still far from standing on my own, but every day was that little step closer.

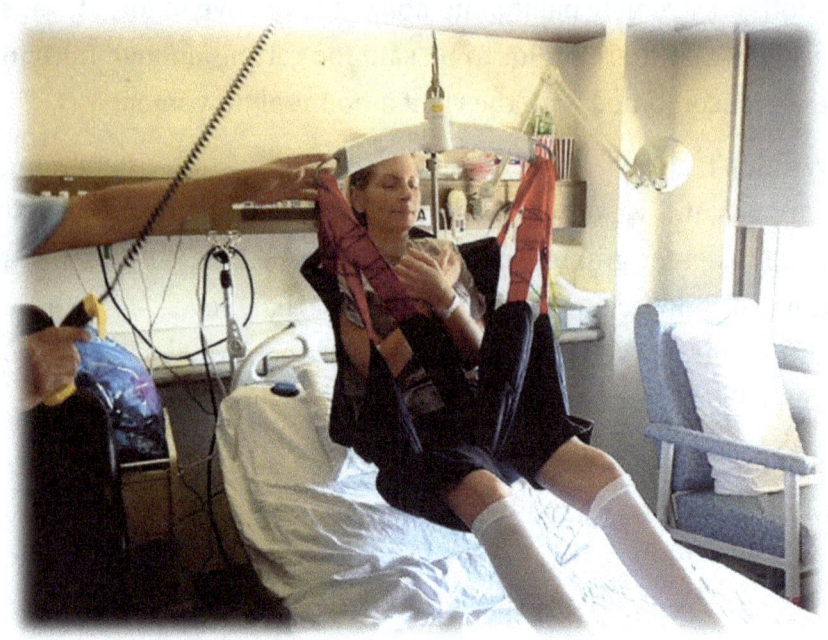

(Ceiling hoist in the Neuro Ward)

SHENTON PARK

After only one week in the Neurological Ward at Sir Charles Gairdner Hospital, I moved to Shenton Park's Rehabilitation Hospital Facility. There were certain criteria to fulfill in order to be admitted as an inpatient with GBS after the acute care from ICU.

I remember the first day was a nightmare. It was like an old-fashioned mental institution with a rundown room consisting of four beds in a very small room with virtually no privacy besides worn-out thinning pull-curtains between the beds. This was certainly not 5-star status, and because the facility was going to be shut down by the end of the year, there was virtually no money being spent on the place. You could tell. It was like going back in time, like a bad movie. I was hoping that I was having a bad dream, but unfortunately that wasn't the case.

My mother was practically hysterical. 'My daughter can't stay here; this is wrong, that is wrong,' she exclaimed with more worry in her face than I've ever seen. In hindsight, it was quite sweet of her to get so frazzled about me staying there, but the hidden blessing in this scenario was that it gave me even more incentive to work that much harder at rehab. The sooner I got better, the sooner I was able to go home.

That light at the end of the tunnel was getting brighter each and every day. This was no place for wimps. The nurses were like kind military sergeants. They had to be. I luckily understood this, and used this as a huge incentive.

My first morning on my own, after sleeping extremely uncomfortably in the worn-out bed, they brought us all breakfast. I hadn't realised how 'delightful' my hospital bed was in the other hospital until I had to lay on this one! I had to use a bedpan at first, which was horrific. I then graduated from a ceiling hoist in the Neuro Ward to a mobile standing hoist. Yippee!

After hoisting me to a wheelchair to sit in, I sat there staring at the food. Due to the muscle wasting and weight loss over the last 8 weeks, I sat like a bag of skin and bones unsupported in a very large generic wheelchair. I could not grip any cutlery, nor could I get it to my mouth yet. The nurses obviously didn't realise this yet, and I sat there and tried to think of a solution to this problem. I did not cry. I just tried to put the piece of toast between my hands, which were like mitts or mittens, and tried to raise it to my mouth. My shoulders were both frozen post-GBS, so I could only rely on a bit of movement from the elbows down. Luckily, that got better with time too.

Fortunately, after my mother and Mark made it a point to get me to a better room, I had a lovely roommate that made the experience almost fun in a comical way. The best part was I was now able to speak and converse! I had my voice back, literally and figuratively. I once again used my focus to not get caught up in the negative things, but instead focused on the positives to keep me on track.

Marina made me a beautiful and inspiring collage of photos to put on my wall next to my bed. Instead of looking at the drab walls and horrible furniture in the room, I focused on that in the morning when I woke up and before I went to sleep.

My parents went on their holiday to the USA. They debated numerous times about leaving me in the condition that I was in, but I insisted that they go and enjoy themselves. This was a blessing in disguise. I had my parents' support in ICU. With the Rehab phase, it was up to me alone to do the work and I had to be super-focused on what needed to be done to assist in my recovery. This was where my friend Stacy and her personal training background proved invaluable, with the assistance in the rehabilitation exercises that made up the majority of my days.

A TYPICAL DAY IN THE REHAB FACILITY

For a total of 3 weeks, the days consisted of getting woken up by a nurse. Then a nurse brought the mobile standing hoist to move me from the bed to the wheelchair. Then we would go down the hall to the bathroom where I would get off the wheelchair (with assistance) and transfer to the toilet to relieve myself from the night.

Showering consisted of transferring from the wheelchair to the shower chair, and eventually trying to get my frozen shoulders and arms to move a bit of a flannel over myself. I still could not stand on my own yet. However, I knew I was getting better as I could wear real clothes and not live in a hospital gown anymore.

I would come back to the room and have breakfast. Mark and Stacy took turns and came every day to help me with mealtimes. I am eternally grateful for them bringing me nutritious food so I didn't have to rely on the less-than-average food that was supplied by the hospital. Their generous nature and selfless attitudes were a huge support for me.

I was measured for a wheelchair that fit my body specifically, and supported my physical structure. One of the tasks that I learned was how to manage an electric wheelchair. I was very excited about this, as I felt my first real step to freedom and independence! I was on my way once I learned how to manoeuvre the joystick on the arm of the wheelchair. That was an accomplishment in itself. I didn't have to rely on anyone to push me, and I felt less like a burden.

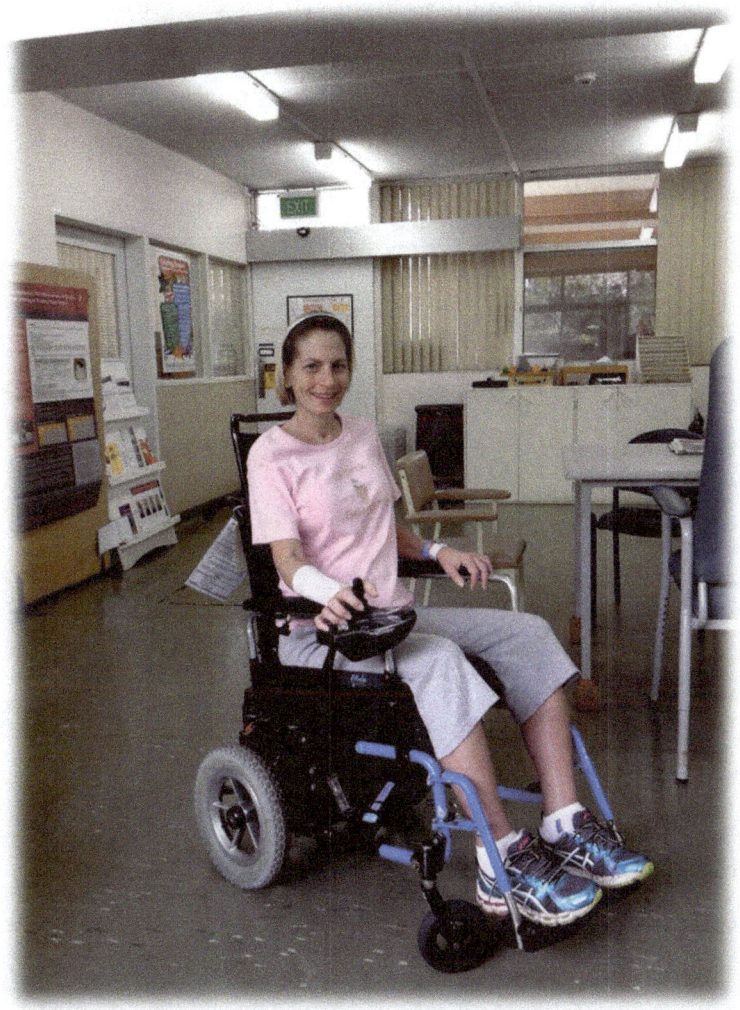

(My electric wheelchair)

Occupational Therapy appointments focused on getting finer movements with the hands and arms. The activities I had to do not only assisted me greatly with my recovery, but I learned so much about the profession and how amazing their work is. Their ingenious tools to get my hands and arms, specifically, back on track were astounding.

(Learning to write again)

I recall one of my tasks was getting up from my wheelchair, taking one step while holding onto the plinth (padded table to sit or lie while performing rehab exercises) and standing beside it, turning pages of a newspaper. I started with one page, due to the restricting pain in my neck and shoulders, and eventually got to ten pages over several days of doing this exercise. The fatigue that followed was indescribable. I quietly thought to myself, "How pathetic! I'm getting excited about turning pages in a newspaper!?!"

(Last days of OT as an inpatient)

I eventually learned to brush my teeth, while sitting in the wheelchair. I also learned to brush my own hair, and eventually washed my face with a washcloth.

Lunch consisted of a healthy meal brought by Stacy or Mark and we usually sat outside in the fresh air and sunshine. This was certainly a highlight of the day. I had prune juice with every meal, due to the side effects of the medications I was still on. I couldn't have survived without it, if you know what I mean.

Looking back, there were a lot of great memories and fun times too. I tried to keep as optimistic as possible and see the bright side of things. We were able to have many conversations, and make up for all of the time I couldn't talk in ICU.

(Learning to pedal a bike again with Stacy by my side)

We would go exploring along the grounds – me in my wheelchair and Stacy or Mark walking alongside me. We would head up to their cafeteria for a treat, or play games that didn't require too much hand movement.

Physiotherapy appointments were daily and this was where the blood, sweat and tears were. Not literally, but I felt a bit like Sylvester Stallone in the 'Rocky' movies with the focus, determination and inner strength to overcome whatever obstacle came up.

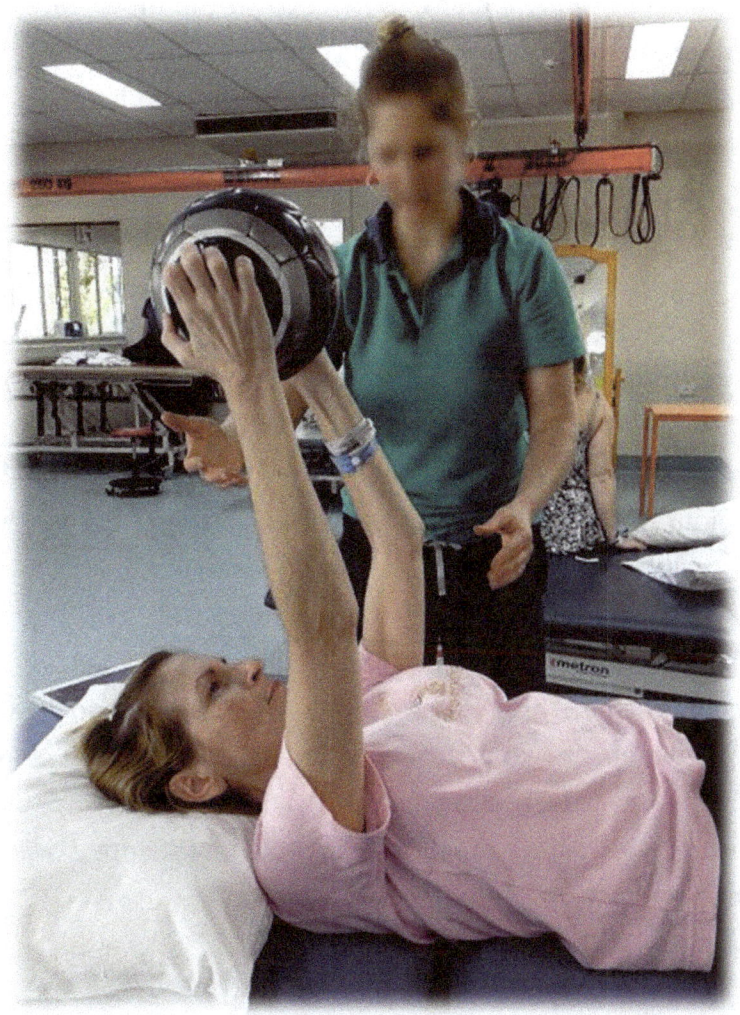

(Developing my arm strength with the physio)

I went through numerous different exercises that challenged my muscles to get back to being able to support my entire skeleton – from my trunk to my limbs to the inner core. Just learning to stand on my own was a scary challenge. I couldn't feel my feet at all when I was learning to do this. I had to 'trust' that they were there and that they would support me. I found that wearing shoes allowed my brain to feel the feet and then I knew they were there. I had to have a pair of athletic shoes one size bigger than usual as my feet were still so swollen from no real movement for over 2 months. The lymphatic system was still continually challenged so lymphatic drainage was an issue. As I could feel the weight of the shoes I tried to feel my legs and train the muscles in my legs and feet to hold me in a standing position. As this continued to get better, after numerous days, I eventually learned to take a step. This was so disconcerting and took so much effort not only physically on my part, but also with an enormous amount of patience on the part of the physios. The last thing I wanted to do was fall, and end up with a broken bone or two to deal with. I had to wear 'Dictus splints' as the nerves were still regenerating and foot drop was still an issue. If I didn't have the splints, I would have tripped over my own feet.

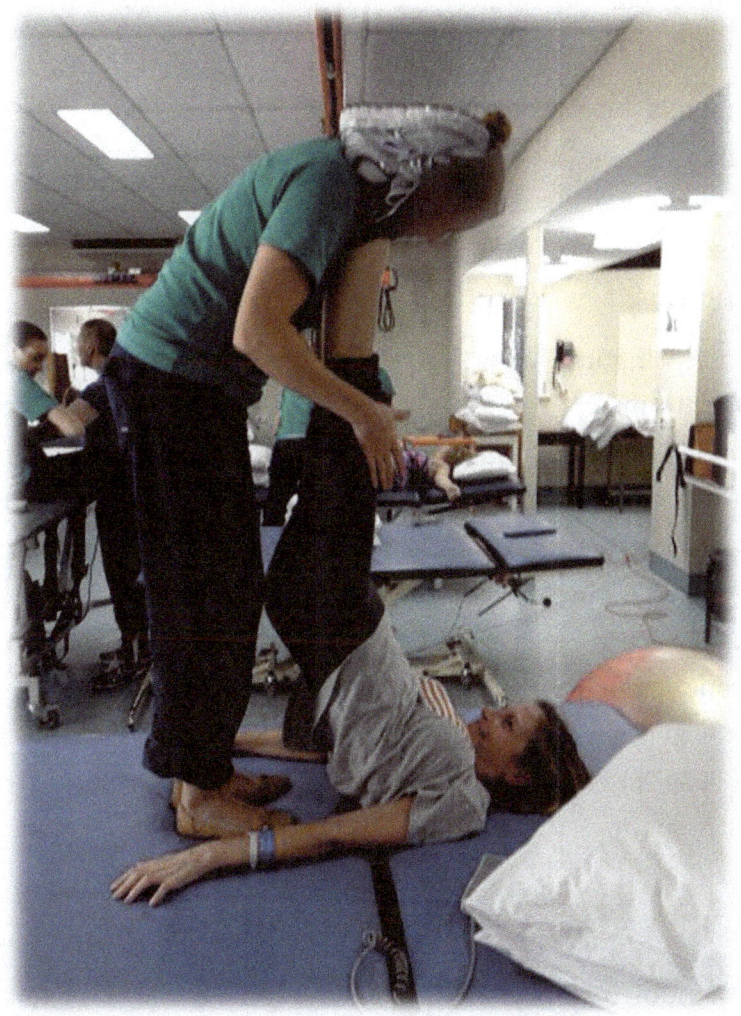

(Developing my leg strength with the physio)

The milestones that were accomplished were so exciting, as small as they technically were. I went from strength to strength, learning and re- learning so many things that can get taken for granted.

Weekends were free – void of appointments. I was fortunate enough to have 'home visits' which started with a few hours one day of the weekend, to one night, to the whole weekend. I focused on all of my OT and Physio during the week. It was my full time job.

It was Springtime in Perth. The weather was lovely, which made getting to my appointments a highlight. I was fortunate here to have access to being outside which I craved so much after being in ICU for 2 months, and only being outside twice in that time. I went in my electric wheelchair to the different appointments which were outside in different buildings, so I was able to stimulate my senses with fresh air, beautiful blue sky, vibrantly coloured flowers, green grass and warm sunshine. This was the hidden blessing of being at the run-down facility that has now closed and been moved to a more sterile environment.

THERE'S ALWAYS SOMEONE WORSE OFF

A standout memory for me at Shenton Park was observing the other patients there. There were so many reminders that we all have issues to deal with. If it's not a physical situation, it's an emotional one. If it's not an emotional situation, it's a mental one. If it's not a mental situation, it's a vocational one. No one escapes challenges and/or hurdles in life.

One patient in particular was a male in his late 20's or early 30's. One day I was in my electric wheelchair heading to an appointment and there was a long stretcher type contraption on wheels coming toward me in the outside corridor. As it approached I noticed this male lying on his stomach, manoeuvering it with his arms. He obviously had no use of the lower half of his body and as he came toward us, he was happily using his arms and smiling and wished us good afternoon.

His attitude, his smile, his energy was infectious. I still get goose bumps when I think of it. Even in his perceived 'unfortunate situation' he wasn't feeling sorry for himself or taking it out on others around him. It was a significant moment to remind myself, 'it could always be worse'. I made a conscious choice to keep my eye on the light at the end of the tunnel, and it did get that little bit brighter each day.

T-REX WITH PANTHER PAWS

This would sum up my existence in Shenton Park. I felt like a T-Rex dinosaur with two arms that were a bit useless as they were close to the body due to very limited range of motion. My hands were like paws in a permanently flexed position where I couldn't grip anything properly.

One day, I had some visitors. My friend Murray brought his little girl, Molly, who was about 5 at the time. She looked at me sitting in the wheelchair with my hands palms up and wondered why I was resting them on my legs with the fingers curled in. After I tried to explain to her that I couldn't move them, she later came up with this clever little statement, 'Dr Pam, you should be a panther for Halloween' and then she tried to mirror my hand movements with hers. My hands were like paws as there was no individual finger movement. This was so sweet, and it has left that imprint in my memory.

SURVIVED: ONE MILLIMETRE AT A TIME

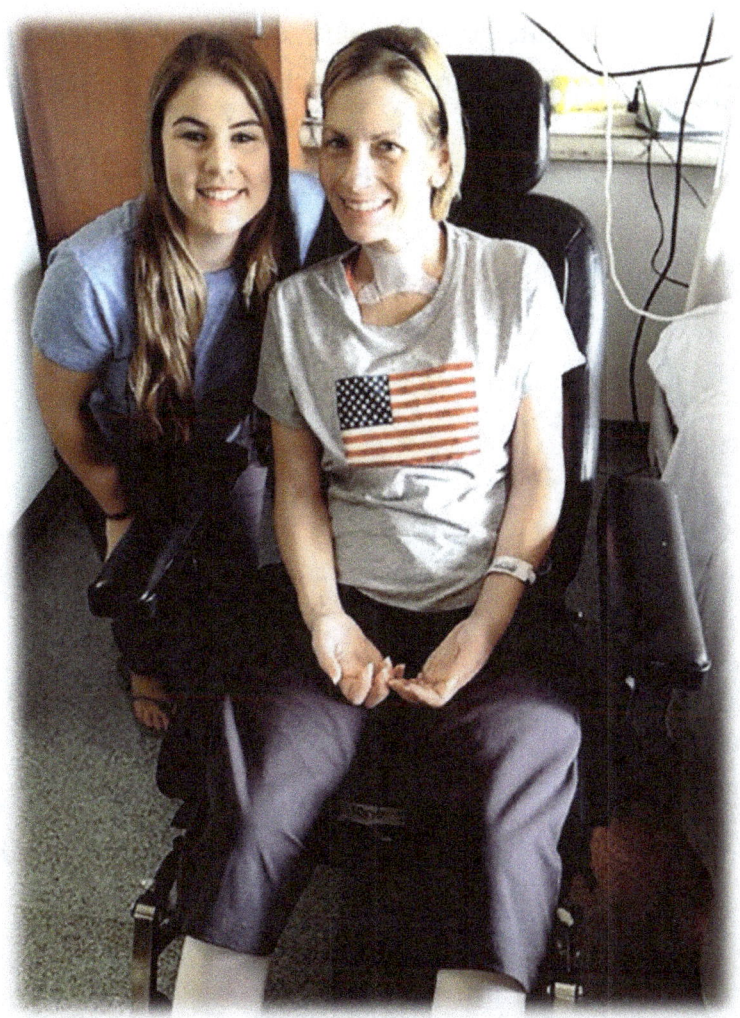

(Marina and T-Rex)

UNPLUGGED

Due to the very limited use of my arms, I also didn't yet have the strength in my hands to even push a button on a remote control. Whilst I chose not to have TV in ICU, Rehab was different. After dinnertime there wasn't much else to do, and I was stuck in my bed. I still required assistance to move, so I ended up watching the programs that were on TV.

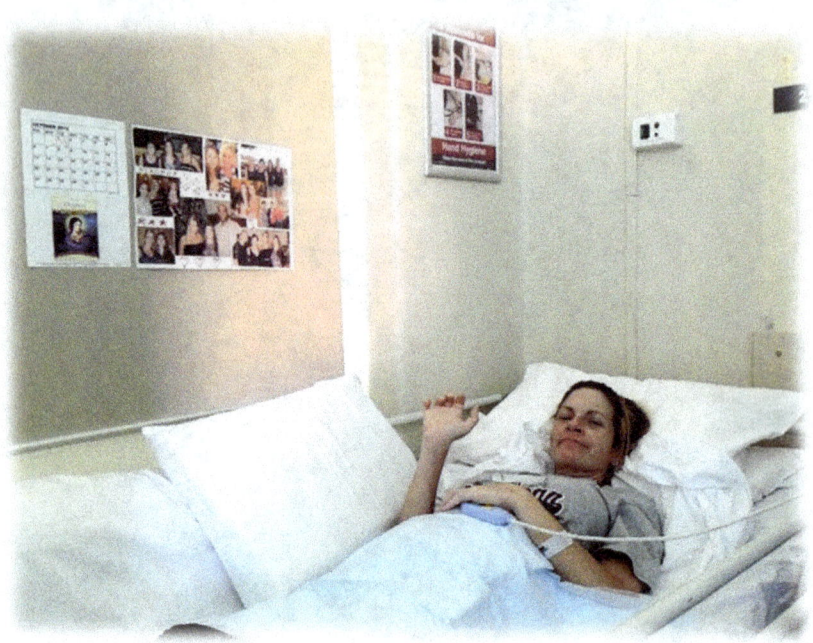

(Evening in Shenton Park Rehabilitation)

I didn't have the strength to change the channel, and I felt bad about getting a nurse to do that, so I just watched whatever was on. I couldn't use my phone, couldn't use a computer, couldn't even hold a book to read. So instead of staring at the wall, I watched the TV above me. This was a revelation in itself! The ability to get addicted to TV shows is astounding. The advertisements are very clever in their marketing as well. I found myself asking Mark to bring me some ice cream that was advertised and he almost fell over. It was so outside my character to ask for ice cream at all, let alone ice cream advertised on TV.

I had a serious break from social media, as I couldn't access it. I looked at this as another blessing in disguise. It was quite liberating and guess what, life still moved on! Yes, we can live without it, and I make a conscious effort now to 'unplug' for either a few hours or even a day over the weekend.

That is another addiction we can get accustomed to. I highly recommend a detox from social media and/or the smartphones that we are so plugged into.

HOME

I was able to return home at the end of October 2013. When I was first admitted to the rehab facility, they did some assessments to determine the length of stay they thought was appropriate for me to be in rehab. They gave me a minimum of

6 weeks after that initial assessment.

I am happy and proud to say that I made it in 3 weeks. I went home in a wheelchair, as I couldn't walk on my own yet, but I was taking steps with assistance and Dictus splints.

The day I was discharged, Mark took me in the wheelchair, picked me up from it and put me into the front seat of our car. It was a glorious day outside, and we drove home along the coast. I distinctly remember having my window rolled down to allow the fresh breezes to come in and blow my hair all over the place. The ocean never looked as magnificent and expansive as it did that day. My senses were so heightened.

I felt like a dog that sticks its head out the window and enjoys the ride. I felt 'free as a bird' after being cooped up for 3 months. Normally, I would never let my hair blow all over the place with the windows down. Times have changed. Tears of gratitude streamed out of my eyes.

I progressed from being an inpatient to being an outpatient of the Rehab Facility. I had an OT and a physio come to my house initially for appointments, and then eventually I went back to Rehab as an outpatient to continue to strengthen muscles, balance and coordination.

Mark became my full-time carer. He was brilliant and selfless, loving and supportive. It certainly was a test to the relationship. This was another thing I am eternally grateful for. Assuming all responsibilities from cooking to cleaning, doing the grocery shopping, to doing laundry, to helping me shower, go to the bathroom – day and night, taking me to appointments. The list goes on and on.

Stacy was there tirelessly by my side through the rehab exercises and milestones. I am eternally grateful for her love and support as well.

Marina and her beautiful heart were selflessly there for me, emotionally and showing true unconditional love, as always. She made sure I was comfortable, helped me to dress, groom and help me feed myself before I could do it myself.

I felt like Dorothy in the Wizard of Oz...after quite an adventure! "There's no place like home."

Chapter Eight – Milestones

"Remember to celebrate milestones as you prepare for the road ahead."
~ Nelson Mandela

After a week in an induced coma, my body was in a state of complete paralysis. Every day I would wait and hope for any sign of movement, meaning my body would be on its way to recovering.

Day by day, any change was a cause for excitement. It was that one step closer to recovering. Every step was significant, as it built on the last. From the first little movement of my index finger, to finally walking by myself on the sand at the beach with the balance, strength and coordination that I had pre-GBS.

This Milestone List may seem a bit over the top, but I wanted to illustrate how each one carried a sense of accomplishment and in turn motivation to keep on going. It meant that I was that bit closer to that light at the end of the tunnel. It meant that I was on my way to achieving the best possible outcome to overcome the effects of GBS.

ICU

Moving the tip of a finger.

Taking a breath unassisted.

Taking a deep breath.

Breathing on own for an hour.

Breathing on own for 90 minutes.

Breathing on own for 120 minutes.

Breathing on own without a ventilator.

Having the trach removed.

REHABILITATION

Keep in mind that the nerves in my upper limbs were recovering first, and functioning before the lower limbs.

Moving the right hand. Moving the right forearm.

Moving the right arm to attempt to wave.

Learning to use the vocal cords.

Learning to speak again.

Swallowing with pain.

Swallowing without pain.

Eating jelly/jello.

Eating pureed food.

Eating and chewing regular food.

Gripping a spoon or fork with foam overlay assistance.

Gripping a cup.

Gripping a cup to bring to mouth.

Holding head up for 30 seconds.

Holding head up for 60 seconds.

Holding head up for 90 seconds.

Holding head up for 120 seconds.

Holding head up for 5 minutes.

Holding head up for 10 minutes.

Sitting on the edge of a plinth (padded table to sit or lie while performing rehab exercises) for 10 seconds without assistance.

Sitting on the edge of a plinth for 20 seconds without assistance.

Sitting on the edge of a plinth for 30 seconds without assistance.

Sitting on the edge of a plinth for 60 seconds without assistance.

Standing with machine for 10 seconds with assistance.

Standing with machine for 20 seconds with assistance.

Sitting on own with assistance.

Sitting on own without assistance.

Standing on own with assistance.

Standing on own without assistance.

THE BIGGEST IMPACT ON ME EMOTIONALLY

Stationary bike with feet strapped to pedals for 60 seconds.

Stationary bike with feet strapped to pedals for 120 seconds.

Stationary bike with feet strapped to pedals for 5 minutes.

Stationary bike with feet strapped to pedals for 10 minutes.

Stationary bike for 2 minutes – unassisted.

Stationary bike for 5 minutes – unassisted.

Stationary bike for 10 minutes – unassisted.

THE SCARIEST YET MOST LIBERATING

Taking walking steps with ankle braces (Dictus splints), with assistance – 3 people.

Taking walking steps with braces, with assistance – 2 people.

Taking walking steps with braces, with assistance – 1 person.

Taking walking steps with braces, without assistance – 3 steps.

Taking walking steps with braces, without assistance – 7 steps.

Taking walking steps with braces, without assistance – 12 steps.

Taking walking steps with braces, without assistance – 20 steps.

Taking walking steps with braces, without assistance – 20 steps, down a driveway.

Taking walking steps with braces, without assistance – 20 steps, up a driveway.

Taking walking steps with braces, without assistance – 20 steps down the driveway, and then 20 steps back up the driveway.

Taking walking steps with braces, without assistance – 20 steps down the driveway, 10 steps down the flat street, 20 steps back up the driveway.

Taking walking steps without the braces, with assistance.

Taking walking steps without the braces, without assistance.

Walking without braces, with a trolley around the house.

Walking without braces, without a trolley around the house.

Walking without braces, without assistance.

Getting up from the toilet with assistance.

Getting up from the toilet by myself.

Going to the toilet, at night by myself.

HOUSEHOLD

Feeding myself with a spoon.

Feeding myself with a fork.

Spreading butter with a knife on a piece of toast.

Cutting food with a knife.

Cooking scrambled eggs on a stove.

Cooking a small basic meal.

Cooking a regular normal meal.

Hanging laundry on the clothesline.

PERSONAL CARE

Sitting on own on a toilet chair over a toilet.

Sitting on own on a shower chair in the shower.

Sitting on own on a shower chair in the shower and using a washcloth over legs.

Sitting on own on a shower chair in the shower and using a washcloth to wash torso as well as legs and arms.

Sitting on own on a shower chair in the shower and washing whole self.

Sitting on own on a shower chair and shaving legs.

Standing on own in shower.

Standing on own in shower and washing hair.

Styling hair.

Putting makeup on.

DAILY TASKS

Holding a pen.

Writing name, legibly.

Writing a sentence, smoothly.

Writing a paragraph in journal.

Pushing keys on piano.

Playing a line of music on the piano.

Playing a song on the piano.

Typing on the computer – 1 word.

Typing on the computer – 1 sentence.

Typing on the computer – 1 paragraph.

Typing on the computer – 1 page.

Typing on the computer – as before GBS.

FREEDOM

Driving the car.

Riding on a bicycle down the street.

Riding on a bicycle, about 500m.

Riding on a bicycle, about 1km.

Riding on a bicycle, 5 km.

Riding on a bicycle, 10 km.

Rollerblading – 1 lap around the rink.

Rollerblading – 10 minutes consecutively.

Rollerblading – 20 minutes consecutively.

Rollerblading – 30 minutes consecutively.

Walking around the neighbourhood, 15 minutes.

Walking around the neighbourhood, 30 minutes.

Walking around the neighbourhood, 60 minutes.

Walking on soft sand beach, 10 minutes.

Walking on soft sand beach, 15 minutes.

Walking on soft sand beach, 20 minutes.

Walking on soft sand beach, 30 minutes.

Walking on soft sand beach, 60 minutes.

BACK TO NORMAL EXERCISE ROUTINE

Using weights, started at 500g and worked up to 5 kg dumbbells (for upper body strengthening exercises).

Achieving full range of motion in both arms.

Hiking, (mild) 30 minutes.

Yoga poses.

Swimming 30 minutes, consecutively.

Water exercise/Water aerobics, 60 minutes.

Doing the splits.

SURVIVED: ONE MILLIMETRE AT A TIME

(Freedom at the top of a lighthouse after cycling there and climbing the steps)

I went from strength to strength, feeling productive and accomplished by ticking off another milestone on my list.

Once those milestones were reached, I felt I had my life back, for the most part.

I felt more human again, not like an alien in a straightjacket hooked up to a bunch of cords and tubes.

Chapter Nine – Up Close and Personal

"Vitality shows in not only the ability to persist but the ability to start over."
~ F Scott Fitzgerald

I had so much trouble deciding on which direction to take with the structure of this book in the early days. The overwhelming mountain of what had happened during my GBS experience left me like a person whose head was spinning after a long roller coaster ride. I had to re-group and equilibrate to get some sort of balance restored. I needed to make sense of it, for myself. I am fortunate to have the wisdom of knowing that it happened for a reason. That didn't make it easy, but it made it worth it.

I came to the realisation that it won't have every single solitary thing I can remember in it, but trust that the words that are meant to be there will be and out of my head. It is not about GBS facts and figures. There are plenty of those out there already. I chose the events and things that impacted me most, intertwined with my most significant memories.

I've embraced the fact that you can't make everyone happy all of the time. Happiness comes from within. And even the word happy can be very subjective. I had my own internal struggles of writing for what I felt others would want to hear or read, versus being authentic – real and raw.

Trusting the timing has been one of my biggest lessons - letting it flow, rather than forcing it to happen. I pushed through numerous stumbling blocks that I now know were 'on the way' not 'in the way'. This little bit of wisdom can be applied to all things in life. That little question to ask yourself when you come across a stumbling block, or what appears to be one: "Is this on the way in my journey? Or is it in the way?"

WHY?

Why was I a 'chosen one' for Guillain Barre Syndrome? Why did it happen to me?

One of the reasons I believe I went through GBS was a crucial part of my spiritual journey and expanding my consciousness. I know this and feel this with every inch of my being. There were so many hidden blessings that were revealed over time. Deep down in my heart, and in my soul, I know that it was the perfect way to get me to stop, slow down and accept things as they are, for what they are.

The ripple effect it has had in my sphere has been nothing short of amazing. I went through it physically, as well as emotionally, mentally and spiritually. Whilst I went through it physically, the people in my life went through it too, mainly on one or all of the emotional, mental and/or spiritual levels, depending on their own journeys.

A thing I could accept early on was that I may never know *how* I got GBS, from a medical standpoint. There are numerous reasons that you can contract it: post infection, food poisoning, exposure to certain viruses, post-vaccines, etc. However, that was one thing I did not get stuck on, as it's not that important to me. What is important is *why*.

INSURANCE POLICY

I'm speaking of two types of insurance policies here.

Firstly, it was advantageous that I had income protection insurance for such a drastic health crisis. I never thought I would need it, but I am grateful that I did. I remember the monthly payments coming out, time and time again, feeling it was a waste of money.

Looking back, it greatly assisted in minimising the financial stress. By eliminating a lot of the financial stress that can be associated with a health crisis such as GBS, the focus can be on recovery and getting back to a healthy state. I can't emphasise this enough.

After all, I was a 'picture of health', eating good nutritious food, drinking lots of water, exercising, doing all the things we are technically 'supposed to be doing'. From the physical aspect, that was a different form of 'insurance policy'.

I believe that if I was *not* maintaining a healthy weight, smoked, drank excessively and was a couch potato, I more than likely would not have had the substantial recovery that I did back to health. Preventive measures are best. If you don't invest in your health, you will be spending on your dis-ease.

That was not where my biggest learning curves were. Health and wellness were already very high on my values. That was not my lesson – it was confirmation that prevention in health and wellness was worth it.

It helped me take it to another level. I appreciate my health more than I ever have, and each day I do my very best not to take it for granted.

CAUGHT UP IN THE SUPERWOMAN TRAP

Admittedly, I was totally caught in the entangled web of the Superwoman Trap. I felt like I had 'nerves of steel' and that I could 'take on the world' juggling numerous things. The pressures that come with it can be overwhelming and we can forget that there can be substantial costs involved – physically, mentally, emotionally, financially.

Potential costs are relationship breakdowns, health crises, for example. The higher stress puts more pressure on your body, especially the adrenal glands nowadays, and that contributes to dis-ease.

I would like to also encourage younger people, especially women, to really be mindful of the symptoms of the Superwoman Trap. I speak from experience, and as I say to my daughter who is a young woman growing up in today's world, use your energy wisely. Spring Free from the Superwoman Trap. Make choices and decisions that are in alignment with your values, not someone else's. Break free from the conditioning that can bind you from being your true self.

MORE LESSONS

The amounts of tears that came during writing my story, re-living the events, the swirls of emotions, the 'movement of my soul' was astonishing.

I was a fiercely independent woman with strongly developed masculine energy. Balancing that masculine energy with more feminine energy has also been one of my life lessons. My GBS journey has been instrumental in bringing that out. As I sit here now with welled-up tears in my eyes, I think that years ago that just would not have happened. I was 'too strong' to cry (so I thought) and not comfortable with that vulnerability.

You don't need GBS to get the life lessons. There are numerous other autoimmune conditions and serious health crises that can afflict. Everyone has a different journey. I wanted to share my story in the hope that it will help and inspire others in some form or another.

It's like a 'lucky dip'. We all come here to this earth to experience events and opportunities to learn and potentially grow from. No one escapes it. It's about how we handle it. We will all have challenges in some form or another. Some will have health issues that appear more serious than others, yet no one can escape challenges in life. Challenges help you grow. You can either: evolve, dissolve, or revolve – going in circles, chasing your tail.

Don't be in a hurry to go 'nowhere' – the rushing around, the busyness, being plugged in and spinning the wheels. There's a lot to be said for being 'still'.

Don't get caught behind the smoke and mirrors (especially via social media) of the 'comparison trap'. Fear of Missing Out (FOMO) seems to have crept into our world with all of the technology we are reliant on. Get to know yourself. Invest in your personal growth and development – what makes you tick, why, what your values are and how you can get the most from your own life.

So if you resonate with one or more of the scenarios, apply them to your own life, as we are all mirrors in one form or another. We have all the traits; some are just more obvious than others.

This has been not only a very physical journey, retrieving my health one millimetre at a time...but a soul journey for me through GBS. I've shared the moments that touched me the most and that are most vivid in my memory. I wouldn't wish it on my worst enemy, yet I can honestly say, it's not only been my greatest challenge but my greatest gift.

Take time to smell the roses, literally. Let people know you love and care about them. Love is the greatest healer and gift of all. Don't take things for granted. You never know when your time is up. Keep your eyes open for the synchronicities that are happening all around us, when we choose to see. Keep your mind open to the magic and mystery life has to offer. No one is guaranteed longevity. Life is short, even when you get a second chance.

"Live for Today ~ Tomorrow will look after itself"

(5 August 2017 – my 4 year GBS anniversary and my parents' 50 year wedding anniversary – causes for celebration indeed!)

"My mission in life is not merely to survive, but to thrive, and to do so with some passion, some compassion, some humor, and some style."
~ Maya Angelou

'Survived' Essentials

The essentials that I used to get me through GBS can be summed up in the following:

S - Support Network (family, friends, Medical & Wellness Teams)

U - Unconditional Love & Understanding

R - Real & Raw – being Authentic – coming back to Self

V - Vision – of your future and appreciating the journey

I - Inventory of what's important; Investment in Self/Health; Integrity of character – no one is guaranteed tomorrow or longevity

V - Values – honouring what's important to you

E - Evolution of inner self

D - Determination – Never Quit, 'Just Keep Swimming' ~ Dory

About the Author

(Dr Pamela Dunn - August 2017)

Dr Pamela Dunn was born and raised in Michigan, USA and has spent the majority of her adult life living in Perth, Western Australia.

She graduated in 1997 from RMIT in Melbourne, Victoria as a chiropractor, and had been practicing right up until the time she was diagnosed with Guillain Barre Syndrome in August 2013.

She has a very keen interest in personal growth and development, and human behaviour. Other interests include photography, music, movies, travelling.

She is committed to maintaining a well-balanced lifestyle – including the application of ancient principles of health, and keeping fit with exercise (walking, swimming, Yoga).

She is a co-founder of 'Perth Photo-Medical Centre' where they use photobiomodulation in the form of low-level laser therapy (LLLT). This assists in the promotion of tissue regeneration and rejuvenation at the cellular level, ultimately resulting in healing, decreasing inflammation and relieving pain in various conditions.

It is her hope and desire to promote GBS awareness, and to inspire others with challenges of potential autoimmune issues on the rise that are affecting the health and wellbeing of people in the world we live in today.

Pamela is currently working on her next book, where she will address all of the specific principles and tools including alternative therapies, exercises, foods, etc. that she used on her road to recovery from GBS.

Connect with Pamela on her Facebook page, 'Survived', and her website: www.survived.com.au

Acknowledgments

To Mark - my 'Superman' husband, my rock, my strong tower. For being there to catch me when I fell, both literally and figuratively. Your middle name is 'unconditional love' and you certainly lived up to that during the entire challenging and continued journey of GBS. I love you, and I am eternally grateful.

To Marina - my one and only daughter. For giving me so many reasons to fight for my life. For being patient and understanding at such a critical time for you in your last years of high school. Your inner strength and love is beyond imagination. You are the apple of my eye - my true pride and joy. My love for you is infinite. I am eternally grateful.

To my parents, Ron & Ceci – I know you would have done anything in your power to take away the pain and suffering I had to endure. You were there for me, every step of the way, with more love and support than I could have ever dreamt of. I love you both, and I am eternally grateful.

To Eric - my brother. For looking after my business affairs; and for being so loving and supportive not only to me, but to the family. We are all stronger because of it. And to my sister-in-law, Shannon, for being by my brother's side during the difficult time and for your love and support. I love you both, and I am eternally grateful.

To Esmat – my angel. For your humble, selfless, angelic nature that brought me inner peace. For the communication with our eyes, as only you could. For dialing into my soul, and bringing me comfort physically through your magic healing hands, and for the healing foods when I could eat. And to Faheem, for driving you all of those nights and for his unconditional love and support. I love you both, and I am eternally grateful.

To Stacy – my Heckle & Jeckle bestie. For helping make the experience 'fun' and memorable as only you could. From the Carillon bowl, to your smiling face and smiling spirit in ICU to the crazy times at Shenton Park. For your selfless assistance in my physio and OT sessions and bringing me fresh, nutritious food every single day when I could eat and regain strength from the inside out. For every unforgettable moment and milestone, you were there by my side unconditionally. I love you, and I am eternally grateful.

To Lucy – my business partner at the time. For looking after my 'other baby' - my patients and chiropractic practice that I put so much heart and soul into. I love you, and I am eternally grateful.

To Raymond – for travelling across the globe to visit me in ICU. I love you, and I am eternally grateful.

To my Patients – I never got to say good-bye, as GBS struck so fast. I felt your prayers and best wishes and I just want to say thank you for your trust in me as your chiropractor, and you all hold a special place in my heart.

To my Family & Friends, near and far - I felt your healing

thoughts and prayers energetically. Thank you from the bottom of my heart.

To Jan Burch, my Editor – for your brilliant skills and your witty conversations through the journey of getting this book out into the world. Reasons... seasons...Thank you so much.

www.ingramcontent.com/pod-product-compliance
Lightning Source LLC
Chambersburg PA
CBHW062243300426
44110CB00034B/1505